Children, Teachers and Learning Series

Series Editor: Cedric Cullingford

Pathways to Literacy

Titles in the *Children, Teachers and Learning* series

Pathways to Literacy

Trevor H. Cairney

CASSELL

Cassell
Wellington House
125 Strand
London WC2R 0BB

215 Park Avenue South
New York
NY 10003

First published 1995

British Library Cataloguing-in-Publication Data
A catalogue record for this book is available from the British Library.
Library of Congress Cataloging-in-Publication Data
[to follow]

ISBN 0–304–32721–2 (hardback)
     0–304–32723–9 (paperback)

Typeset by Chapter One (London)
Printed and bound in Great Britain by Biddles Ltd, Guildford and King's Lynn

Contents

Foreword

The books in this series stem from the conviction that all those who are concerned with education should have a deep interest in the nature of children's learning. Teaching and policy decisions ultimately depend on an understanding of individual personalities accumulated through experience, observation and research. Too often in recent years decisions on the management of education have had little to do with the realities of children's lives, and too often the interest shown in the performance of teachers, or in the content of the curriculum, has not been balanced by an interest in how children respond to either. The books in this series are based on the conviction that children are not fundamentally different from adults, and that we understand ourselves better by our insight into the nature of children.

The books are designed to appeal to *all* those who are interested in education and who take it as axiomatic that anyone concerned with human nature, culture or the future of civilization is interested in education – in the individual process of learning, as well as what can be done to help it. While each book draws on recent findings in research and is aware of the latest developments in policy, each is written in a style that is clear, readable and free from the jargon that has undermined much scholarly writing, especially in such a relatively new field of study.

Although the audience to be addressed includes all those concerned with education, the most important section of the audience is made up of professional teachers, the teachers who continue to learn and grow and who need both support and stimulation. Teachers are very busy people, whose energies are taken up in coping with difficult circumstances. They deserve material that is stimulating, useful and free of jargon, and is in tune with the practical realities of classrooms.

Each book is based on the principle that the study of education is a discipline in its own right. There was a time when the study of the principles of learning and the individual's response to his or her environment was a collection of parts of other disciplines – history, philosophy, linguistics, sociology and psychology. That time is assumed to be over and the books address those who are interested in the study of children and how they respond to their environment.

Each book is written both to enlighten the readers and to offer practical help to develop their understanding. They therefore not only contain accounts of what we understand about children, but also illuminate these accounts by a series of examples, based on observation of practice. These examples are designed not as a series of rigid steps to be followed, but to show the realities on which the insights are based.

Most people, even educational researchers, agree that research on children's learning has been most disappointing, even when it has not been completely missing. Apart from the general lack of a 'scholarly' educational tradition, the inadequacies of such study come about because of the fear of approaching such a complex area as children's inner lives. Instead of answering curiosity with observation, much educational research has attempted to reduce the problem to simplistic solutions, by isolating a particular hypothesis and trying to improve it, or by trying to focus on what is easy and 'empirical'. These books try to clarify the real complexities of the problem, and are willing to be speculative.

The real disappointment with educational research, however, is that it is very rarely read or used. The people most at home with children are often unaware that helpful insights can be offered to them. The study of children and the understanding that comes from self-knowledge are too important to be left to obscurity. In the broad sense real 'research' is carried out by all those engaged in the task of teaching or bringing up children.

All the books share a conviction that the inner worlds of children repay close attention, and that much subsequent behaviour and attitudes depend upon the early years. They also share the conviction that children's natures are not markedly different from those of adults, even if they are more honest about themselves. The process of learning is reviewed as the individual's close and idiosyncratic involvement in events, rather than the passive reception of, and processing of, information.

Cedric Cullingford

Introduction

I am grateful for having been given the opportunity to write this book by Cedric Cullingford and Naomi Roth. Each book one writes has its own special pleasures and difficulties. This book has been notable because of the difficulty I have had just getting started. I revised the outline several times before finally settling on the content which follows. Writing a book is always painful because of the emotions it stimulates – frustration, apprehension, inadequacy, lethargy and, most insidious of all, fear. Do I have anything new to say? Will my readers like what I have to say? Will I like it when it appears in print? These are just a few of the questions that arise.

But enough of this; as you can see, I am still avoiding finishing this book!

The title of the book, *Pathways to Literacy*, has evolved from dozens of other alternatives. The word 'pathways' encapsulates much of what I believe about literacy learning. My reasons for including this word in my title are simple. One of the clearest lessons that I have learned in my 25 years as an educator is that there is no single pathway to literacy learning. Indeed, there are probably as many pathways as there are literacy learners, because we all learn to be literate in rich social contexts as we engage in unique sets of human relationships. If we believe that literacy is socially defined and sustained (and I do), then almost by definition we must accept that all will come to literacy in slightly different ways. It is also worth noting right at the outset that literacy is hardly a unitary social practice. Once it would have been defined as the ability to read and write, but now we would want to define it more broadly. One definition is that literacy is the ability

> to read and use written information and to write appropriately in a range of contexts. It is used to develop knowledge and understanding, to achieve personal growth and to function effectively in our society. It also includes the recognition and use of numbers and basic mathematical

> signs and symbols. Literacy involves the integration of speaking, listening, reading, viewing, writing and critical thinking.
>
> (Australian Language and Literacy Policy)

While some would think that this is too broad, it recognizes the interrelationship of reading and writing with other ways of knowing, and goes some way towards acknowledging the social and cultural nature of literacy.

When one adopts broad and complex definitions of literacy it leads one to different practices in the classroom. Teachers who define literacy narrowly (e.g. as simply the learning of reading and writing skills) will create different classrooms from those created by the teacher who recognizes that literacy is a term that covers a multitude of cultural practices.

In this book I want to explore many issues. I begin in Chapter 1 with an attempt to define literacy more fully and to explore its social dimensions. In this chapter I suggest that we learn to read as an extension of human relationships, and then examine the sociocultural foundations of literacy. I then provide an overview of the reading and writing processes and examine key research. The chapter then explores the way in which meaning is socially constructed. Finally, it considers how literacy is essentially cultural practice.

Chapter 2 examines the concept of community as a metaphor for describing how classrooms might be established. It examines the way in which people learn to be literate as they relate to and interact with each other. In doing this I explore the intertextual nature of literacy experiences, and provide an insight into how this operates in classrooms.

Chapter 3 is an important chapter because it explores the essential relationship between the student, the teacher and the text. It explores at length the work of Rogoff and Vygotsky, and explains how this work affects the essential nature of the roles and practices that we sanction in our classrooms.

The creation of effective literacy environments is the subject of Chapter 4. It attempts to demonstrate through the description of several classroom contexts how environments can be created that are consistent with what we know about the nature of literacy and learning.

Chapters 5 and 6 attempt to outline how we can implement strategies in classrooms that lead to the development of avid readers and writers. These chapters attempt to show how an understanding of the nature of literacy as cultural practice leads to the development of different classrooms that acknowledge that there are many pathways to literacy.

In Chapter 7 I attempt to show how assessment and evaluation are integral to teaching and learning. I describe a teaching and learning cycle that can be used to develop authentic assessment practices in classrooms.

Chapter 8 is concerned with programming. I provide an overview of basic steps to programming and then attempt to provide an insight into how programmes can be developed that enable the ideas of the first seven chapters to be implemented.

In the final chapter I address a number of tough questions. These include seeking justice and literacy for all, the place of technology in today's classrooms, and the need to develop effective partnerships between schools and their communities. These issues are examined in order to leave the reader with one broad overarching question: how do we ensure that all children have access to the literacy practices that are needed to succeed in their world?

I trust that you will be challenged by the ideas that I offer in these nine chapters. If you reach the end of this book having tussled with the questions that I raise, then I will be well pleased.

I believe that all teachers need to address a range of issues in the 1990s. I feel privileged to have been able to share my thinking with you. I am also grateful to the many people who have influenced me: my colleagues around the world; the many students with whom I have worked; my postgraduate students who challenge me regularly; the many parents whose ideas have enriched my life and my academic work; and finally, my family, Carmen, Nicole and Louise Cairney, who tolerate me and keep my feet firmly planted on the ground.

Trevor Cairney

CHAPTER 1

Towards a sociocultural understanding of literacy

Prior to the 1980s the field of literacy was dominated by psychological research and theorizing. The last decade, however, has seen the emergence of an interest in the social dimensions of literacy, particularly in how it is socially constructed. Literacy (for many) is no longer viewed simply as a cognitive skill. Rather, it is seen also as a cultural practice. As Haas Dyson (1993) points out, literacy learners are seen as 'social negotiators', exploring and exploiting the power of symbolic tools like literacy as a form of social mediation. Literacy is used as a cultural tool to construct symbolic meanings and to engage with others. It is also acquired as people relate to one another.

This shift, from reading as a cognitive process to reading as a complex cultural practice, has been dependent on a number of differing influences. The early 'psycholinguistic' work of scholars such as Goodman (1965, 1967), Harste (Harste *et al.*, 1984) and Snow (1983) was instrumental in creating an awareness of the need to consider the child in real world contexts. Also, the work of psychologists like Vygotsky (1978) and Bruner (1986), in highlighting the importance of the relationship between the skilled and less skilled learner, provided further impetus to the consideration of the relationships that exist in classrooms and their role in supporting literacy development.

Sociolinguistic theories of language derived from writers like Bakhtin (1935/1981), Gumperz (1986), Halliday (1975) and Hymes (1974) also played a major role in this shift. These theories built upon the basic understanding that language is made as people act and react to one another. From this were derived a number of key related constructs. First, people learn to be literate primarily in groups as they relate to others to accomplish social and communicative functions. Second, literacy is purpose-driven and context-bound. Third, people react to the actions of others as well as to set patterns of group interaction. Fourth, people may act and react to each other through sequences of actions, not just single acts. These actions primarily involve language (of which literacy is obviously a part) and related semiotic systems (e.g. group membership, school organizational frameworks and so on).

Similarly, literary theory played its part by challenging long-held views concerning the centrality of text, and its presumed location. Writers like Iser (1978) described the text as a set of incomplete instructions to be completed by the reader as gaps are filled as part of a constructive and predictive process. Eco (1979) in turn pointed to the unlimited meanings that readers generate when faced with a text.

More recently, the work of poststructuralists has had a strong influence on the move from notions of literacy skill to those of literacy practice. This work grew essentially out of the work of structuralism (e.g. Saussure, 1974) and has argued that people actively take on specific discourses through which they (and others to whom they relate) shape their world. This will be discussed in more detail later in the chapter.

The combined and overlapping impact of these quite disparate scholarly traditions has been to bring about a significant shift in the way we define literacy. It is clear that one learns about literacy within a social context, as an extension of relationships with other people. Hence, the meanings we create as we read and write are always relative. What we think we know can never be removed from the social context within which we have come to know (Cairney, 1990a, 1990b). All texts are implicated in social relations. We learn to read and write by 'being apprenticed to a social group' (Gee, 1990, p. 45).

It is apparent that the meanings we construct as we read and write reflect who we are, what we have experienced, what we know about language and the world, and also our purposes for creating them in the first place (Cairney, 1990a, 1990b). Types of discourse and the way we read or write them are the social constructs of specific groups. Individuals are enculturated into these practices and these meanings. These ideas will be elaborated later in the chapter, but first it is important to focus more closely on the reading and writing processes.

The emergence of the study of the reading process

Since the early 1960s our knowledge of the nature of the reading process has increased dramatically. In the 1940s and 1950s a great deal of attention was given to reading methodology. But this was to change with the rise of psycholinguistic theories and their challenges to traditional wisdom concerning the psychology of reading.

Perhaps the greatest stimulus to this debate was Goodman's early work on miscue analysis (Goodman, 1965, 1967). Goodman challenged the notion that reading was a precise and sequential process driven by decoding. Instead, he suggested that it was in a sense a highly constructive process which he referred to as a 'psycholinguistic guessing game'. Goodman and other educators (e.g. Smith, 1971) stressed the importance of reader-based factors in the reading process. In particular, the role of background knowledge was stressed, with it being theorized that reading is a process dependent on both reader and text-based factors driven by the reader's search for meaning. Goodman suggested that rather than comprehension being dependent on sequential text processing, it begins with reader-based attempts to make meaning which lead to the sampling of print to confirm or refute the reader's predictions. This search for meaning, he suggested, is aided by the reader's implicit knowledge of orthographic redundancy.

The work of cognitive psychologists concerned with schema theory (see Schallert, 1982, for a useful summary) provided further stimulus to the development of new knowledge concerning the reading process. In particular, the work of the staff and postgraduate students of the Center for Reading (University of Illinois) pushed the field's understanding of reading forward. The 1970s saw the development of a number of interactive theories that attempted to explain how reading works. Essentially, these 'top down' models of reading placed greater importance on the reader's knowledge and suggested that reading is context-driven, with readers using existing semantic and syntactic knowledge to aid predictions about the print. In this way, it was suggested, only print actually necessary is sampled and decoded.

In the late 1970s and early 1980s this work was extended further by theorists who developed 'transactive' theories of reading (e.g. Rosenblatt, 1976; Eco, 1979; Shanklin, 1982). Using insights gained from literary studies, semiotics, and linguistics, this work attempted to move beyond simple definitions of how texts were comprehended. These researchers proposed that reading involves a transaction between a reader and a text which leads to the creation of a new text that is unique to each reader. Rosenblatt (1976), for example, suggested that meaning is always greater than the potential meaning residing within the reader or that which the author attempted to communicate.

These theoretical positions which reflect constructivist notions of knowledge and how it is derived are in stark contrast to code emphasis models (e.g. Gough, 1972; Perfetti, 1985) which hypothesize a 'bottom up' view of reading. Reading is conceptualized in such theories as being driven by the sequential processing of print. While those supporting this perspective accept that background knowledge has an influence, they reject the suggestion that it drives meaning making and the reading of text. Rather, it is suggested that readers process virtually all text, and that reading is a modular process, dependent on rapid and automatic word identification, rather than context.

In recent times, these views have been given some support by eye movement research (e.g. Just and Carpenter, 1980; Ehrlich and Rayner, 1981; Balota *et al.*, 1985), which has suggested that readers do in fact process print more systematically and comprehensively than previously suggested by psycholinguists like Goodman. In fact, this work suggests that with the exception of very high frequency words (e.g. 'and', 'the') readers process all words, and in fact all letters within them. While it is difficult to substantiate that readers do process all print on which they fixate, the evidence does nonetheless suggest that the development of automaticity in decoding is important to reading. Questions have also been raised concerning the extent to which readers use context when reading (e.g. Nicholson, 1991). Nicholson has questioned the validity of Goodman's (1965) conclusions and claims that context is not as substantial an influence as originally claimed. Nicholson attempted to replicate Goodman's early research (Goodman, 1965), which required students to read words in context then to read them later in isolation. He concluded that the effect of context was not as pronounced as claimed by Goodman, and that reading was far more text driven than had been theorized.

However, in spite of these debates concerning the extent to which reading is dependent on automatic decoding and the serial processing of text, it is universally agreed that reading is a complex meaning-based process requiring the interaction of text and reader-based factors.

The emergence of writing as a 'serious' pursuit

Historically, interest in writing was primarily concerned with the written product rather than the writing process. It was not until the 1970s that the first serious attempts were made to examine the writing processes of children. As Wilkinson (1986) indicates, very little research was done at all on writing in education until the 1970s. Initial interest in writing research had its roots in the late 1960s and early 1970s. This was a period of intense interest in 'creative writing' with numerous teacher ideas books being published. This work had its theoretical beginnings in the work of Hartog (1907), who argued that writing is essentially a means of developing thinking. It was also encouraged by the publishing of a number of influential writers' anthologies with accompanying commentary (see Wilkinson, 1986, for a discussion of these texts).

The period from the mid-1960s to the mid-1970s saw a number of developments which represented the beginnings of more focused study of writing in schools. In this period Moffett's (1968) classic text *Teaching the Universe of Discourse* was published and the work of Britton, Stratta, Dixon, Rosen, Barnes and Wilkinson created the climate for significant advances. One of the first great steps forward came with the funding of the largely descriptive research projects *Writing and Learning Across the Curriculum* (Martin *et al.*, 1976) and *The Development of Writing Abilities* (Britton *et al.*, 1975). From this work emerged a concern for purpose and audience and the development of one of the first attempts to describe the writing process. Using the developmental data generated by their work Britton *et al.* (1975) postulated their now well-known (though largely disputed) theory that expressive writing (personal writing like speech written down) was the source from which other forms of writing developed.

A significant turning point in writing research came in the early 1970s as the first research projects to focus on the writing process began to emerge The key initial works were published by Emig (1971) and Stratta *et al.* (1973). Emig described the composing processes of eight students by asking them to compose aloud. This work led Emig to conclude that the composing process has a number of key dimensions: the stimulus; a pre-writing phase; starting to write; composing aloud; reformulation; stopping; contemplation of the product; and teacher influence on the piece. Stratta *et al.* (1973) described workshops on writing in which teachers wrote in response to specific experiences. The participants were asked to reflect on their writing in relation to themselves as writers and also their students. This work was the beginning of numerous teacher discovery writing workshops and projects that developed in the English-speaking world, the most famous being the Bay Area Writing project. This early work was followed by more intensive study of the writing process by English educators as well as cognitive psychologists (e.g. Scardemalia and Bereiter, 1983).

Running parallel to this interest in writing was a renewed interest in spelling. Similarly, this was characterized by a concern for the processes involved in spelling, something that was in stark contrast with decades of methodological research. Some of the most influential work was conducted by Chomsky (1970), Read (1975), Harste *et al.* (1980) and Harste *et al.* (1984). This research emphasized that spelling is an integral part of the composing processes of writers and was able to describe a range of strategies used by writers beyond the use of phonological and orthographic processing.

It was against this backdrop that the process writing movement began. This renewed interest in writing reached its height in the early 1980s as teachers were challenged to consider writing as process rather than just product. It was Graves (see Graves, 1984 for a detailed summary of his early work) who was to take the interest of researchers and educators and turn it into a revolutionary movement that swept schools throughout the English-speaking world (and later many non-English-speaking countries). Perhaps more than anyone, Graves took research on writing into classrooms. Prior to Graves' work one could well argue that only Emig (1971) had spent long periods in classrooms actually observing the composing processes of young writers. What Graves offered was the first detailed description of what children did and said as they were engaged in the writing process. Graves not only examined the products of writing, he observed children as they wrote and talked about their writing.

Since this work was all conducted in classrooms, and involved the development of a range of methodological procedures, the work was quickly adaptable for ordinary classroom use. As a result, Graves' research was quickly turned into a series of practical publications for teachers (e.g. Graves, 1983) and spawned a range of other teacher-as-researcher publications which continue to influence classroom practice (e.g. Turbill, 1982; Atwell, 1987; Calkins, 1991). One of the most significant developments from this work was the growing integration of reading and writing. As writing theorists and researchers began to examine the writing process closely, they began to realize that there were many parallels with reading (Shanklin, 1982; Tierney and Pearson, 1983; Cairney, 1985), and in particular that both were constructive or 'composing' processes. This in turn led to an emphasis in research on literacy. From the early 1980s we saw the emergence of integrated studies of how children engage in reading and writing. The work of whole language researchers like Harste *et al.* (1984), Cambourne (1988) and Dyson (1989, 1993) has done much to extend our work in this way.

The increased interest in writing, while stimulated by researchers like Emig (1971), Stratta *et al.* (1973), Scardemalia and Bereiter (1983) and Graves (1983), soon had associated problems with teaching methodology as the orthodoxy of process writing was born. This was ironic because the last thing that researchers like Graves were aiming to produce were new orthodoxies to replace the old. Rather, the purpose had been to challenge teachers to become observers of their children who could make informed curriculum decisions based on their detailed understanding of the children's writing processes. With this also came an artificial distinction between process and product and a reluctance on the part of teachers to intervene in children's writing. Critics of these practices (e.g. Christie, 1990) quite rightly point to the folly of assuming that a child-centred curriculum means that students are to be left to discover written language by themselves. However, any such critics need always to acknowledge the context within which process writing was born. That is, one where the writing curriculum was teacher centred, was dominated by 'one-shot' draft writing, and was associated with the decontextualized teaching of spelling and grammar (Walshe, 1981). The process writing movement was an attempt to break down these less than helpful practices. These issues will again be raised in Chapter 6.

The social construction of meaning

What is clear about literacy is that one learns about it within a social context, as an extension of relationships with other people. Hence, the meanings we create as we read and write are always relative. What we think we know can never be removed from the social context within which we have come to know (Cairney, 1990a, 1990b). All texts are implicated in social relations. We learn to read and write by 'being apprenticed to a social group' (Gee, 1990, p. 45).

The meanings we construct as we read and write reflect who we are, what we have experienced, what we know about language and the world, and also our purposes for creating them in the first place (Cairney, 1990a, 1990b). Types of discourse and the way we read or write them are the social constructs of specific groups. Individuals are enculturated into these practices and these meanings.

As we make meaning in reading and writing we do so in relationship to other people. This chapter was not written in a vacuum, nor will it be read in a vacuum. What I have written and what you will understand as a process of your reading reflects who we are and the groups into which we have been socialized.

Read the following short text and reflect on its meaning. If possible discuss it with a colleague or friend.

I need less week and more weekend.

What does this text mean? The short answer is that it can mean many things to many people. Of course the context will help to constrain meaning. I have this text written on a small sign that sits on a shelf next to my study desk. If one was to read it in a financial newspaper one might think that it was a rather nonsensical text which runs counter to prevailing wisdom concerning the need for the full utilization of plant and personnel in order to increase productivity. On the other hand, it might be seen as a radical attempt to re-create a committed workforce by increasing leisure and promoting job sharing. These explanations, however, are less plausible given the fact that the text begins with 'I', which indicates that it is meant to be a statement by an individual about themselves.

Most people living in Western cultures would fairly quickly see that this text is in fact a light-hearted attempt to appeal to our belief that we are overworked in our modern world. However, this may well be a rather confusing statement for some cultures, which demand almost continuous employment for survival. Even within our own Western culture it would not have the same impact for those who are unemployed. Rather than leading to amusement, it might simply highlight for them that they need work and would gladly give up all leisure to obtain it. Such a text might extract anger rather than amusement.

The text has a different impact for those people who are not only employed but who tend to be workaholics. It has special significance for me because it was given to me by my family. In a sense they were making a very clear statement to me about my work practices and their desire to spend more time with me. Clearly, the full impact of this text is very much dependent on its specific context.

Our reading of this simple text highlights a number of things about the social constructiveness of literacy:

- Readers and writers create meaning, they don't simply transcribe, summarize or extract it.
- The meaning readers and writers create is always 'greater' than the written text's potential meaning and the literacy user's prior knowledge and experiences.
- No two readers or writers can ever read or write the same text in the same way; nor do they arrive at the same meaning as part of these processes.
- Above all, meaning is relative, socially constructed, and only relevant within the context of the social purposes and relationships to which the reading or writing is directed.

Beyond simple definitions of literacy

We acquire specific literacy in rich social contexts as we engage in unique sets of human relationships. Because literacy is socially defined and sustained, individuals come to literacy in slightly different ways.

I will refer a great deal in this book to *literacy practices* rather than simply *literacy* to avoid the tendency we have to assume that literacy is a unitary skill which we either can or cannot use. Like some other literacy educators, I will argue that literacy is not a single unitary skill (Gee, 1990; Luke, 1993; Welch and Freebody, 1993). Instead, it is defined as a social practice which has many specific manifestations. There are many forms of literacy, each with specific purposes and contexts in which they are used. Literacy cannot be separated from the people who use it. To understand literacy fully we need to understand the groups and institutions in which we are socialized into specific literacy practices (Bruner, 1986; Gee, 1990).

In contrast, there have been teachers and literacy educators whose practices have been driven by narrow skills-based notions of literacy. Indeed, in the past decade we have seen some attempt to define literacy as a commodity, able to solve most of our economic problems if we can only manage to introduce it to those in need. However, while success in school literacy may enhance educational and life chances, it is not the magic panacea for the economic and social ills of the 1990s. In fact, Graff (1987) has suggested that the traditionally accepted wisdom that literacy leads inevitably to achievement, higher-order thinking ability, social growth and personal empowerment is little more than a myth.

In this book there are a number of overarching questions that drive the very nature of the ideas and practices that I explore. Why is it that school literacy disempowers some, and empowers others? How must schools change in order to ensure that literacy is empowering for all? What types of classroom environments permit all children to gain access to the literacy practices which they need to take their place in the world? In addressing the latter, let me say at the outset that I will not simply be suggesting new methods. While I have contributed my share of books and papers on methodology in recent years, I believe that we have spent too much time arguing about teaching methods. I have been persuaded by writers like Shannon (1989) that much of our debate over literacy methods is not simply centred on a concern for the literacy practices of our children. Nevertheless, I will attempt to provide an overview of the diverse classroom practices that I believe are necessary to permit students to acquire literacy in all its fullness.

As Gee (1990) points out, schools engage in particular discourses. To be a teacher in any school demands specific ways of using language, behaving, and interacting, and adherence to sets of values and attitudes.

We need to recognize that the definitions we hold of literacy are inevitably reflective of a specific ideology and, as a consequence, arbitrarily advantage some while disadvantaging others (Street, 1984; Freire and Macedo, 1987; Lankshear and Lawler, 1987). As Scribner and Cole's (1981) work showed, literacy *per se* does not necessarily lead to cognitive growth and development. Rather, they found that what matters is not literacy as an isolated skill, but the social practices into which people are enculturated (or apprenticed) as members of a specific social group. In other words, one gets better at specific social practices as one practises them. Furthermore, those children who enter school already having been partially apprenticed into the social practices of schooling (of which literacy is a part) invariably perform better at the practices of schooling right from the start.

What is to be our response to this observation that schools, and teachers as their chief agents, act as 'gate keepers'? How do we respond to the claim that 'short of radical social change' there is 'no access to power in society without control over the social practices in thought, speech and writing essay-text literacy and its attendant world view' (Gee, 1990, p 67)? Gee suggests that English teachers need to accept their role as socializers, and reflect critically, comparatively and with a 'sense of the possibilities for change'.

Such ideological thoughts are almost anathema to teachers who want to get on with the everyday practices of teaching. But the challenge of these ideas cannot be denied. Some, when faced with the call for revolutionary changes in society (as suggested by some critical theorists), want to run and hide. Others want to take up the revolutionary challenge. Still others ask cynically 'What do revolutions achieve anyway? Didn't Illich try to change society by getting rid of schools?'

Schools are among the most stable institutions in society, and short of a total transformation in the society within which they are embedded, they will not be moved quickly. However, move they must. My response to this reality is not to keep telling schools that they need to change (this does little other than further privileging the 'tellers'), but rather to engage in social evolutionary development by providing opportunities and alternative practices which challenge existing educational practices. This is clearly one of the purposes of this book.

Language is a complex human endeavour

As my discussion has already made clear, in recent times there have been serious challenges to narrow skills-based definitions of literacy. One of the major changes that occurred in the 1980s and early 1990s has been a broadening of definitions of literacy. These new definitions typically recognize the relationship of reading to writing, accept that literacy has many forms beyond the book, and view literacy as a social and cultural process rather than just a cognitive skill.

As I have stated already, many now choose to talk of 'literacy practices', a term which recognizes that there are many literacies. This term reflects the recognition that literacy is crucial to much social activity, and is interconnected with other cultural practices and specific contexts (Cairney and Langbien, 1989; Cairney, 1990a, 1990b). Literacy is embedded in culture and contributes to the shaping of it.

We need to resist the tendency to simplify definitions of literacy and, in the process, reduce it to little more than a technocratic skill. The desire to incorporate outcome measures into curriculum documents is just one way in which we run the risk of assuming that language can be reduced to a series of competencies that can be taught, presumably in some kind of developmental sequence.

Of course we know that we can produce lists of competencies, but when we do, what our students produce in the name of English language has little purpose that will be life transforming. I can recall little of my early primary school literacy experiences. In fact, the only memory I have of the whole of my first grade year is of being harassed by a teacher because I could not sound out a simple word. Now it is interesting to reflect on this ordeal. I was asked to stand in front of a class and attempt to sound out a word I knew well – 'nest'. While I had trouble handling the final consonant blend, I could recognize the word and say it. Interestingly enough, at the time I had an aviary in my back yard that contained 200 birds and many nests, and I spent much of my recreation time climbing trees to collect eggs (yes, from nests!) to add to my collection (a practice I have long ago discarded as ecologically inappropriate). Such pastimes were common in my community when I was growing up.

My teacher's well-intentioned desire to show me how to sound out the word 'nest' had only a negative effect on me as a person and literacy learner. The literacy practice that she was insisting that I master had little relevance to my world.

I would like to contend that, when teachers impose limited definitions of what it is to be literate on their students, many inappropriate demonstrations of literacy are offered. This in turn can lead to similarly inappropriate literacy practices.

Literacy is a cultural practice

Literacy as we know it is a cultural practice. It is inextricably interwoven with the culture of our children. It refects culture (the beliefs, values, ideas and knowledge of a group of people) and in turn helps to shape it. As Heath (1983) demonstrated, what counts as literacy is intertwined with culture. Gee suggests that it is almost impossible to separate literacy practices from other cultural practices. Literacy is 'part of the very texture of wider practices that involve talk, interaction, values and beliefs' (1990, p. 43).

We know, for example, that not all cultures value books in the same way. In fact, we know that not all sub-groups within a given society place equal value on literacy. But even this statement can be misleading, because what is closer to the truth is that not all people have access to or value the same literacy practices.

This is problematical. For example, schools often hold the assumption that all the cultures our schools interact with value literature in the same way that middle-class white native English speakers do. Similarly, in recent times there has been the same cultural arrogance shown concerning the importance of specific written genres (see Cairney, 1992b; Cairney and Munsie, 1992a for a fuller discussion). On the surface we assume that all students need access to the same written genres as middle-class teachers. This manifests itself in a range of equally inappropriate teaching practices. We set restricted reading lists for Senior Secondary English classes, we reject particular texts which are not seen as ideologically sound, we assume that our students will need to use the text forms that we value as vehicles for learning.

I was confronted with this reality two years ago while working with young people (aged 12–24 years) in gaols and youth detention centres in Western Sydney (Cairney *et al.*, 1993). These contexts were observed as part of a funded Federal Government research project which sought to 'develop and evaluate literacy programmes suitable for young people held in institutional care'. Within this project we attempted to meet the literacy needs of young offenders (aged 15–25). But how are you to meet the needs of prisoners who do not value what the teacher sees as literacy, who cannot see how it could empower them, who think about little else except getting out to loved ones, their next 'job', and keeping their 'noses clean' while inside? Which text is more significant to the prisoner, the letter from a partner, or a vocational training manual? Which genre is more empowering, the poetry of resistance, or a Letter to the Editor?

As Lemke (1993, p. 18) points out, written language has developed in practice 'around only one dialect of spoken English, the upper-middle class sociolect' which is unnatural for most learners. How do we respond to the observation that the literacy practices of schooling are restrictive (see Luke, 1988; Baker and Freebody, 1989; Gilbert and Taylor, 1991 for further discussion)? Even the very texts we provide for children represent only a limited part of our shared cultural experiences.

We know also from classroom-based research that the treatment teachers give to children can vary along racial and class lines. For example, Oakes (1985) found that the specific graded class a student ended up in was influenced more by race, class and family background than by general intelligence. Similarly, Rist (1970) found that the instruction of African American children in kindergarten, first and second grades was influenced strongly by the teacher's implicit judgement of the ideal classroom learner. Furthermore, these judgements were based on social information (e.g. cleanliness and 'interest') rather than academic information.

Even in the everyday functioning of the classroom it seems that critical decisions are made which limit some children's opportunities for learning. Research has consistently shown that a child's social class has a strong influence on the way teachers talk to and respond to children's reading and writing, how groups are set up in classrooms, the volume of literacy opportunities offered, the difficulty and interest levels of reading material provided, and so on (see Cairney, 1987a for a fuller discussion).

In the nineteenth century the dividing line between the literate and non-literate was defined by culture and class. In the 1990s the dividing line in 'developed' countries between those who are empowered by literacy and use it to control their world and those who tend to use it for a more limited range of purposes defined by others is still typically class- and culturally-based. And, in the 'under-developed' countries, the pattern is still that of the last century. Gee suggests that literacy has always been used 'to solidify the social hierarchy, empower elites and ensure that people lower on the hierarchy accept the values, norms and beliefs of the elites' (1990, p. 40).

This presents a conundrum for us, because we know that the

language of the privileged empowers. Some will be inwardly arguing now that we have a responsibility to introduce children to the language of the middle-class.

To quote Margaret Meek (1991):

> Everyone knows that to be at home in a literate society is a feeling as well as a fact. We are aware that, in our history, literacy has exalted the poor to the level of the powerful. John Bunyan, the tinker, influenced the thinking and feeling of his time more than archbishops. In the lives of ordinary people across the centuries literacy has had importance beyond its usefulness, beyond its function in public networks of social cohesion and the techniques of its production. However, and wherever people learn to read and write, literacy adds to their sense of human worth and dignity. Most people agree that we extend our consciousness, our sympathies and our understanding in the ordinary process of reading a newspaper or a novel, or by writing a letter of condolence. Because we can read we can also question the authority and the apparent dominance of those whose forcefully written documents urge something upon us. We can query the gas bill. We write as well as speak to register our protest against injustice. By learning to read we gain knowledge. In writing we come to ask ourselves what it is that we know and understand, so that we too can go 'on the record'. So we take for granted the fact that, in our society, we and our children need to be literate. At the same time we should understand that literacy, so natural-seeming to us, is not universal. There are still places in the world where people do not learn to read and write in childhood because their way of life does not depend upon it. To be 'non-literate' in these places is therefore not a term of defect or of deprivation. (pp. 3–4)

How do we respond to these issues and anomalies as teachers? One response is simply to suggest major societal change to remove social injustice and inequality. Few seriously believe that this is easily accomplished; social change is inevitably slow. Another response is to recognize the cultural variation that characterizes the communities in which we work and as a consequence seek to introduce new practices and new relationships with students and their families.

The work of researchers like Heath (1983), which has illustrated the way culture and literacy practices are interwoven, leaves us with a dilemma. If we accept that schools cannot realistically change at a pace out of step with broader society (some would argue that they should and must, whereas I am less than convinced that this could occur easily), we are faced with the realization that if students who are not socialized into the discourse practices of schooling are to succeed they must eventually be socialized into them if they are to acquire the literacy practices that will ultimately empower.

So what is my response to this dilemma? It is to take the middle road. While some might question this road, I believe it can be travelled. What I am suggesting is that we must continue to seek reform of schools and society, breaking down the privileging of a limited range of literacies, and attempting to recognize multiple literacies. As part of this process, however, we have a responsibility to introduce children to the literacy practices that do offer the greatest potential for educational success, employment, and personal empowerment. The conundrum that we face, however, is that this very middle ground might simply serve to more firmly establish the limited discourses of those who are currently empowered and privileged.

As I said at the outset, we need to be less concerned with debates over methods, schemes and procedures, and more concerned with the interactions and relationships that we permit and encourage in our classrooms. Also, we need to constantly reflect upon the discourses we promote in the classroom and the extent to which individuals are empowered or disempowered by the discourses we privilege.

The central question that drives my practice is, how can I empower students to use literacy for ends which they see as relevant and legitimate? In the chapters that follow I intend to address this concern.

CHAPTER 2

Making connections: the importance of community to literacy learning

In this chapter I want to explore the importance that a recognition of the social nature of literacy has for classroom practice. I want to argue that the type of interactions and relationships that you permit, and indeed encourage, will make a difference to the literacy learning of your students. I want to make use of the concept of 'community' because it represents a useful metaphor for describing the type of classroom environment that I am advocating.

Building communities of readers and writers

The following description is of observations within the classroom of one of my postgraduate students. The literacy events that are described provide an insight into the nature of this community of learners, and how this affects literacy learning (Cairney and Langbien, 1989).

The observations begin as Susan is reading to her kindergarten children. Nineteen small four-year-old faces were looking up at her as she chatted with them about the story 'The three little pigs' (Jacobs, 1969). The children were sitting cross-legged on a large carpet square at the front of the room, the venue for news, music, discussion, sharing ideas and, last but not least, stories. The group had been asked to comment upon the story and was responding enthusiastically. Ideas flowed quickly as the comment of one child stimulated other responses. The discussion moved from one part of the story to another. Different characters were mentioned, and favourite parts shared.

Sometimes the comments related closely to the story, at other times they were more egocentric. Their attention turned to the big bad wolf and Robert announced:

I've got a big bad wolf and I put him in hot water.

Louise replied:

My bad wolf got shot with hot rocks.

Christian responded with a somewhat deeper thought:

The wolf got hurt because he tried to hurt the pigs.

These young children were part of a small community of language users who were delighting in the sharing of reading and writing. The kindergarten children were attending a kindergarten in a small town set among the canefields of far north Queensland (Australia). The buildings were modest and the fittings and equipment fairly standard. There was a nature table in one corner, large and small building blocks, easels, paints, clay, and a reading corner which is physically appealing. The reading corner included a brightly covered divan, a few cushions, a variety of books, newspapers and magazines. A sign was hanging on the wall asking 'Have you read any good books lately?' Artwork displays also showed the influence of literature, and group craft efforts to depict characters from books were proudly on show.

The teacher in this classroom (Susan Langbien) had been actively attempting to develop a community of readers and writers. As one observed the room it was plain to see that literacy was an important part of the world of this class. Each session of the day included the reading of a piece of poetry or prose. Frequently, these sessions were followed by lively discussion. Daily independent reading time was provided on the carpet area. News time frequently involved the spontaneous sharing of books. Opportunities were provided for response to reading, and this took many forms – drawing, writing, dramatic re-enactment, mime, and singing.

Even when the teacher was not initiating reading or writing, the classroom was filled with literate behaviour. In the dress-up corner several children were including story reading in creative play. Children took turns as mother reading to her baby. Genevieve was asking her pretend mum to explain why the dog in *I'll Always Love You* (Wilhelm, 1985) had such a sad face. Mum was doing a wonderful job explaining the relationships within the story. Another group playing shops was using a receipt book to record purchases. Receipt books were often referred to in the home corner. 'Mum' and 'dad' were reading the newspaper and later flicking through the pages of the telephone book.

This classroom was living evidence of the complex social nature of literacy. A teacher and her class were talking, listening, reading and writing as parts of a dynamic community. Literacy was being learned as children related to each other, meaning was being created within a complex community of relationships. Susan's classroom demonstrated many of the social elements of literacy that I want to explore in the rest of this chapter.

Knowledge, thought and learning are intrinsically social or collaborative (Kuhn, 1970; Vygotsky, 1978). One cannot discuss the reading and writing processes without recognizing the inherent social aspects of these processes. The recognition and acceptance of literacy as a social process should change us and empower us as teachers to transform our classrooms. It should enable us to create classroom environments where children take control of their own learning. This view of literacy should lead to fresh insights, and different teaching methods, methods that recognize that literacy is inherently social.

Reading and writing involve social relationships

A concern for the social nature of literacy should lead to a recognition that reading and writing events involve social relationships. Bloome (1985a) suggests that

> reading involves social relationships among people: among teachers and students, among students, among parents and children, and among authors and readers. The social relationships involved in reading include establishing social groups and ways of interacting with others; gaining or maintaining status and social position; and acquiring culturally appropriate ways of thinking, problem solving, valuing, and feeling.

Susan's class was being introduced to the world of literacy in an environment where it was valued. Reading and writing were being shared and enjoyed, as an extension of close relationships (teacher-to-child, child-to-child). Whether inside the classroom or in the playground, reading and writing often found their way into the language of the group. For example, at morning tea Christian began to chant:

> Wombat stew, wombat stew, crunchy munchy for my lunchy, wombat stew. (from *Wombat Stew* [Vaughan, 1984], a book that Susan had shared)

Other children soon joined in and pretended their morning teas were lizards' eyes, a cane toad, mud and slime and a crocodile's tooth. A new and complex 'socially' constituted wombat stew was created. As they played they not only relived the experience of the book, they learned about language.

Meaning is constructed in a social context (Halliday, 1975, 1978) and, in turn, language learning is dependent upon social relationships (Snow, 1983). Snow examined the language interactions of parents and children in the pre-school years, and found development was facilitated in a number of ways. First, adults often continued or elaborated topics that the child introduced. Second, they reduced the uncertainty in the language task by structuring the dialogue. Third, they insisted that their children complete language tasks (e.g. answer the question) if they thought they knew the answer.

The development of reading and writing are dependent upon similar procedures and are an outgrowth of a social interaction process. Thomas (1985) studied fifteen early readers and found Snow's observations for spoken language were true also for reading. Parents, grandparents and older siblings in her sample answered numerous questions concerning print, pictures and text. They also constructed pre-reading, during-reading, and post-reading questions to help facilitate meaning. Finally, parents expected their children to recognize print in a variety of settings, and expected them to read words consistently in a variety of contexts.

The above arguments leave us as teachers with a lot of important questions. Is literacy learning a social and collaborative process in our classrooms? That is, are the social relationships within the classroom facilitating or impeding literacy development? To answer this, we need first to recognize that it is impossible for teachers to stop language learning from being an intrinsically social and collaborative process. However, it may be that while your students are learning from each other via the 'underground curriculum' (Dyson, 1985), everything you do as a teacher within the 'real' curriculum involves little collaborative learning.

In an earlier piece of research (Cairney, 1987b) I found that, while children may show little commitment to school literacy tasks, they frequently use literacy for their own purposes, as part of the network of relationships present within their classrooms. I found that notes were passed, posters were designed advertising a Cabbage Patch Kid club, signs were posted on desks warning others to leave things alone (or risk 'broken faces'), joke books were shared, music was read (and enjoyed), and so on. Reading and writing were being used for functional purposes.

It seems that the interactions we permit and encourage in our classrooms make a big difference to the literacy development of our students. The way we organize our classroom physically (grouping arrangements, provision or non-provision of communal workspaces, etc.), the way we control interactions (e.g. do we insist on children raising hands whenever they speak, do we allow movement in the room, etc.), the role we play in the classroom (are we participants/learners, or directors and teachers?) all make a difference to the learning that occurs in our classrooms. Issues such as these are just as important as decisions concerning teaching methods.

We need to ask, can independent reading, literature-based programmes and 'process writing' (i.e., programmes based primarily upon the work of Donald Graves) operate effectively in classrooms where the teacher does not recognize the social and collaborative nature of learning? The answer is *no*! For example, implementing the procedures required for an independent reading programme, without permitting students to share their reading with others, or allowing them to respond in an atmosphere of trust and warmth, will be doomed to failure. What we need to do as teachers is create environments which permit the sense of collaborative language learning that the children in Susan's class were experiencing within their classroom.

Reading and writing as extensions of day-to-day activities and relationships

While the learning of language and the learning of culture are different, they are nevertheless interdependent (Halliday, 1975). Language is itself a cultural phenomenon. As Bloome (1985a) points out, all communication is cultural, and involves shared means of acting, feeling, believing, and thinking. Reading and writing in turn are cultural activities. Both have social uses which are an extension of people's day-to-day cultural lives.

The playground in Susan's kindergarten was often the setting for much child initiated drama and dramatic play. Little birds looked for their mothers (from *Are You My Mother?* [Eastman, 1960]). A group of children became the Three Billy Goats Gruff and the troll, and used a balance beam as their bridge. Another group played 'house' and whenever Genevieve set off for the shops she reminded herself *Don't Forget the Bacon* (Hutchins, 1976).

We need only to examine our own lives to see how writing is a part of our culture. It emerges as a natural part of our lives. As we go about the business of our day we jot down friends' phone numbers, addresses, and birthdays. We send cards, apologies, requests. We make statements, maintain relationships, make demands, and try to persuade.

When we read we also do so as an extension of our daily lives. We read certain types of books to impress our friends ('Have you read…?'). We use books as a pretext to open conversations. Some people read Mills & Boon romances as an extension of their relationships – a fantasy for some, an escape for others. People carry their Bibles with them as they go to church, sometimes to read, sometimes just as part of their Sunday attire. Some line their walls with books to impress people, and prove they are 'real' intellectuals.

The place of books as an extension of our culture extends even to the creation of 'secret codes'. For example, the teacher who is annoyed with a student announces 'You're a pest, you're a menace…', to which another student responds 'You cannot live here'. This becomes a common line used in the room for the rest of the year. The experience of sharing *Lester and Clyde* (Reece, 1976) has been significant, and a special line has become one of the secret messages which is only of importance to members of this class, because it is part of its shared culture.

Another phenomenon which occurs frequently within Susan's classroom is something Keifer (1983) calls a 'grapevine' response. Frequent subjects of the class grapevine are books with special features. For example, *Aranea* (Wagner, 1979) has a page filled with a spiral spider web the children love to trace their fingers around. *The Very Hungry Caterpillar* (Carle, 1969) has holes to count, poke and peer through. The grapevine quickly operates as children discover these fascinations and wait anxiously for a turn to read the story.

All teachers need to ask themselves: to what extent is reading and writing a positive extension and shaper of the culture of my classroom? how significant is literacy within the life of my classroom? how important is it within the lives of the children I teach?

The social construction of meaning

In Chapter 1 I argued that meaning is constructed within rich social contexts. In essence, classrooms are places where students encounter a complex range of texts which interact with one another as students, read, write, view, say or listen to them – that is, an 'intertextual' world of constantly interacting meanings.

The concept of intertextuality is simply the process of interpreting one text by means of a previously composed (read or written) text (Barthes, 1979; de Beaugrande, 1980; Kristeva, 1980). Most people if probed will indicate that they frequently think of other books as they read. Similarly, many writers freely admit that the germs of their writing can often be traced to previous literary experiences with texts written and read (Cairney, 1990b, 1990c).

Margaret Mahy (1987) was well aware of her intertextual history. When reflecting upon her childhood literary experiences she commented as follows:

> I wrote because I was a reader, and wanted to relive certain reading experiences more intimately by bringing them back out of myself... books give me access to a continuous and reciprocating discussion, and the awareness of lots of things all going on simultaneously, a concurrence that seems to me to be an important aspect of truth... I think I dissolved the books I needed and no doubt I still carry them (in solution) within me. (pp. 151–7)

The concept of intertextuality is in a sense a metaphor used to describe the constant social construction and reconstruction of meaning, as readers and writers 'transpose texts into other texts, absorb one text into another, and build a mosaic of intersecting texts', (Hartman, 1990, p. 2).

In previous publications I have described students' awareness of their intertextual histories, its impact upon them as readers and writers, and the way this is manifested in classrooms (see Cairney, 1988a, 1990b, 1990c, 1992a). It was concluded from this research that intertextuality is:

- idiosyncratic
- dependent on factors as diverse as text characteristics, reading purpose, contextual influences, etc.

- something of which most readers and writers are aware irrespective of age and ability
- linked with many text features including genre, plot, characterization and content
- frequently primed by specific elements of content and plot (Cairney, 1985, 1988a, 1990c, 1992a).

However, what is of greatest relevance to the discussion in this chapter is, how do intertextual meanings develop, and what is the role that others play in any individual's process of making meaning? Data from a detailed case study of a grade 1 classroom (students aged 5–6 years) shed light on these questions. These data concern just one form of intertextuality: links between texts read by the teacher and student writing. But this form of intertextuality is common within classrooms.

In 1987 I began visiting a grade 1 (5–6-year-old children) class taught by Inta to observe the literacy behaviour of young children (see Cairney, 1990c and 1992a for further information). Inta was an experienced teacher well respected by students, colleagues and parents. She was a committed teacher with a strong interest in language and literacy. On the first day in Inta's classroom I observed a boy named Brock eagerly writing in a 'magic cave' constructed as a retreat area. I stopped to ask how he came up with this idea for his story. He replied:

> Well, it was like Chlorissa. That book [*The Enchanted Wood*] had children who moved to the country. I changed it around.

Brock's piece based on the *The Enchanted Wood* (Blyton, 1939) was primed (at least in part) by the fact that Chlorissa had done this earlier. Similarly, Kylie, who wrote a poetry book titled 'A rocket in my pocket', decided to pursue this writing as a response to an exchange with a friend. Although the title (at least) of her poetry book was inspired by the Dr Seuss book *There's a Wocket in My Pocket* (Seuss, 1974), her decision to write it emerged as she talked about writing with a friend. As I observed her writing I stopped to talk about her piece:

T.C.   So, why did you write a poem today?

KYLIE.   Because my partner said I could write a poem – we're going to make a book.

T.C.   Where did you get the idea from?

KYLIE. Because we need a story about it.

T.C. Who needs it?

KYLIE. My partner and I. I used the first line then made up the rest.

All literacy events are in essence social (Cairney and Langbien, 1989). Kylie and Brock's use of prior texts was influenced and shaped by the complex relationships between participants in this literary environment. This was in essence a case of 'stolen' narrative. But unlike a normal case of theft, what is stolen is not the actual object; rather, it is its essence or 'echo'.

As pointed out in Chapter 1, we learn as we relate to other people and acquire literacy as an extension of the relationships we build with others. The choices we make as literacy learners, our literary preferences and our interests are all inextricably linked with the relationships that characterize our world.

This was evidenced strongly in this grade 1 classroom, and was reflected, for example, in student preoccupation with Enid Blyton's 'Faraway Tree' books. These students' teacher had read two of these books (*The Enchanted Wood* and *The Magic Faraway Tree*) in the first four weeks of school. The third (*The Wishing Chair*) was read over a two-week period some two months later.

The books are a series of adventure stories involving a group of three children (Jo, Bessie and Fanny) who move to the English countryside. As they explore their new environment, they discover a special forest (the Enchanted Wood) and within it a tree with magical powers (the Magic Faraway Tree). The children are involved with a group of fantasy type characters living in or around the Enchanted Wood (e.g. Silky, Moon Face, Dame Washalot, Angry Pixie), and a series of magical lands that change daily, and are entered through a hole in the clouds by climbing the Faraway Tree.

The teacher's reading of these books had a strong influence upon the writing of children in the classroom. This showed itself in the students' narrative writing, in playground games, in letter writing and even at home. In all, ten 'Blyton type' stories were written in this classroom during the year. The first major piece of writing was produced by Amanda (aged 5 years) during a single week in March. This piece was titled 'The Enchanted Wood' and was a retelling of the first two chapters of Blyton's (1939) book of the same name. It was typed by an aide and published for other readers within the class. Following is part of the story:

The Enchanted Wood

Once there was three children and their Mum and Dad. They lived in the cottage in a wood. One day their Mum said they could have a free day because they would work hard the next day. They knew there was a wood behind their cottage. Then they had an idea they would go the wood and off they went. Then they couldn't find the Faraway Tree. Then they remembered something. If they whistled three times they would find the Faraway Tree. Soon one brown pixie came out of the woods and took them to the Faraway Tree and Silky brought some pop biscuits and we went up to moon faces and moon face said 'come up to the top of the tree it is "supper land"'. Bessie said 'Lets go up and stay with moon face'. So then Jo, Bessie and Fanny climbed up the tree.

While Amanda and Sally's stories were the first major pieces, there had been a number of smaller pieces of writing that referred to the 'Faraway Tree' books, including notes to Inta and to friends. One month later Sally wrote a story based on *The Magic Faraway Tree* (Blyton, 1943). This appeared after the second Blyton book had been read. It was eventually published in June.

The Magic Faraway Tree

There were three kids. There names was Nikki and Leanne and Adam. Nikki is the oldest. They went to live in a little cottage. It was very nice. They looked over the house and saw a forest. Then they went out of the door and went to the forest and saw a big tree and they went to climb the tree and climbed up and up very high and they found some friends. Their names was Moon-face and Silky. Moon-face had some pop biscuits and google and some toffee shocks. There was lots and lots.

The end.

The next story to appear was Chlorissa's draft which she began in June and was still writing at the end of the school year (December). By this time the story was twenty pages long. On the same day that Chlorissa began her story, Brock began a piece based on *Adventures of the Wishing Chair* (Blyton, 1937). Brock wrote for approximately twenty minutes in the 'magic cave', but the piece was left abandoned at the end of the day. Brock never returned to it.

In August, Nikki was first observed writing a piece about some children who were lost in a magic wood. Like Chlorissa, she was still writing this fifteen-page piece in December. Her story showed clear links with *The Enchanted Wood* and was largely a retelling. Within the text, she substituted her own name and the names of friends (Lauren, Sarah, Ben) for Blyton's characters.

Shortly after Nikki began her story, Alice began a piece called 'Fanny and her friends'. While this piece used one character, Fanny, and the setting of the Enchanted Wood, the story line is essentially her own. She finished her six-page epic one month later.

Lauren began her 'Faraway' piece several weeks after Nikki. It had only limited ties with the Faraway Tree stories, featured a series of mysterious doors each of which offered opportunities for adventures, and had an intrusion of pixies, witches, etc. She finished this story three weeks later.

Kathleen began a story in early September which was essentially a rewrite of several adventures in different lands discovered at the top of the Faraway Tree. This piece was not completed until early December and eventually was over six pages long.

Sarah also started a Faraway piece in September. This was primarily a retelling of Blyton's (1937) book *The Wishing Chair*. The draft of this piece was lost two weeks later, and Sarah abandoned the story.

In late October Alice began a second story (shortly after finishing the first). She exclaimed as I watched her:

> I'm writing another Faraway story and this one is going to have the whole class in it!

This piece was filed away that day and not touched again. This was the last major 'Blyton type' piece to begin, although Nikki and Chlorissa continued writing until the end of the year, and many other informal references to the Blyton books were made through letters, posters, etc.

What emerges from a close analysis of the Blyton influence on writing in this classroom is that the rise of Blyton lookalikes was a natural outgrowth of a specific group interest shared by members of the class. The writing of these pieces grew out of relationships with their teacher and fellow pupils. The three Blyton books provided the opportunity for a significant group literary experience.

From the time Inta began reading the books there was complete class involvement. Everyone found it hard to wait to find out what was going to happen next. Each day's reading was eagerly awaited. In between readings children talked about the story, and reference was made to the book in numerous notes from children, which were a natural part of the class letter-writing programme.

When viewed from this perspective intertextuality will always be viewed as social and inseparable from the contexts of which it is a part. Any act of reading or writing is a response to other acts – an 'ongoing dialogue' – as people act and react to each other.

I will argue in the following chapters that social dialogue about text is an integral part of the learning of literacy. One would expect that the creation of classroom contexts that facilitate opportunities for students to interact with other students in order to develop more elaborate socially constructed meanings would have an important effect on the literacy learning of students.

Conclusion

I started this chapter by describing the environment that Susan had created within her school, a classroom dominated by literate behaviour. Her children read and wrote as natural extensions of their lives. They learned to read and write as they shared relationships with each other. As they did, they learned from their world what it means to be literate, and soon found that reading and writing not only provide pleasure, but are important for many of the purposes of life. Susan was aware that the type of literacy environment she created was vital, and that her place in it was critical. She had set out to create a community that valued reading and writing and that used these processes as a natural part of the world. The major challenge for all teachers (like Susan) is to create classroom environments in which all children come to value reading and writing as natural extensions of their lives. We need to give our students a place where they share and grow as members of a literate community. Such classrooms help students to build intertextual histories. Teachers need to create literacy environments in which reading, writing, and talking about reading and writing occur as natural extensions of the relationships that bind the members of classroom communities together. One of the teacher's most significant functions is to stir the 'cauldron of stories' (Tolkein, cited in Cooper, 1988, p. 7) that make up the collective intertextual history of our classrooms. That is, we need to create classrooms that are rich in textual meanings.

In Chapter 3 I want to explore this idea more fully and consider how teachers should create literacy environments which promote the literacy development of students.

Note

Parts of this chapter have appeared in two separate previous publications: Cairney and Langbien (1989) and Cairney (1992a).

CHAPTER 3

The teacher, the student, the text

The purpose of this chapter is to look more closely at the relationship between the teacher, students and the texts spoken, listened to, viewed, written and read in classrooms. As I have stressed in Chapters 1 and 2, reading and writing are learned as people relate to each other using language (as well as other sign systems). Classrooms are filled with talk, which has numerous functions, audiences and forms. The teacher's role is a key one, both as frequent 'talker' in the room and as a facilitator of 'text talk', that is, talk about the texts written, read, viewed, experienced and heard in classrooms (Cairney, 1990b, 1992). What follows is an attempt to explore more fully the role that teachers play in classrooms as joint constructors of text. To do this, I want to examine three complementary themes which have a strong bearing on the role that teachers play in classrooms. The first is the complex relationship between language, teaching and learning, the second is the way in which students are 'apprenticed' into ways of thinking and using language and literacy, and the third is the role that questioning plays in student learning. In the light of these intersecting themes I will then discuss the way teachers should talk about texts in their classrooms.

The relationship between language, teaching and learning

As has probably become clear from the first two chapters in this book, much of my thinking has been strongly influenced by the work of a number of writers and researchers who have examined the relationship of language (and of course literacy) to education. The first group of largely English researchers developed its work primarily during the 1960s and 1970s (e.g. Britton, 1970; Barnes *et al.*, 1971; Bernstein, 1971, 1973; Edwards and Furlong, 1978; Halliday, 1978; Green, 1979). The work of these researchers and writers (and others) marked the beginning of a strong concern for language and teaching as more than simply separate objects of study. Rather, these researchers began to examine teaching and learning as communicative processes, and language as a personal resource and a social construct (Green and Dixon, 1993). This concern with the relationship of language to learning was enhanced by a clear interdisciplinary focus, with the work of English educators, psychologists, sociologists and linguists being integrated to an extent not previously seen within the field of language and literacy education.

In the 1980s and early 1990s there was a continuation of this work (e.g. Stubbs, 1980, 1983; Green and Wallat, 1981; Heath, 1983; Meek *et al.*, 1983; Cochran-Smith, 1984; Harste *et al.*, 1984; Bloome, 1985b, 1987; Wells, 1986; Cazden, 1988), with further interdisciplinary extension into anthropology, semiotics, and historical research. This phase of the development of research in this area saw an increased interest in the sociocultural nature of language and literacy, and challenges to our preconceived notions of how language is constructed.

I want to argue in this chapter that it is important to recognize that oral and written language, while linguistically different, are nonetheless intricately interwoven with each other in the life of the classroom. It is virtually impossible to read or write in classrooms without talking. Conversely, talking often leads to reading and writing. Spoken and written language are closely related aspects of classroom discourse.

While this is a book about literacy, it has been argued in Chapter 1 that literacy is a sociocultural process. That is, one learns about literacy within a social context, as an extension of relationships with other people. All texts are implicated in social relations. We learn to read and write by 'being apprenticed to a social group' (Gee, 1990, p. 45). Hence, the meanings we construct as we read and write reflect who we are, what we have experienced, what we know about language and the world, and also our purposes for creating them in the first place (Cairney, 1990a, 1990b). Types of discourse and the way we read or write them are the social constructs of specific groups. Individuals are enculturated into these practices and these meanings as they read, write and talk about reading and writing.

The classrooms in which teachers and students live each day are 'interactionally constituted'. That is, 'classroom life is constituted in and through the patterns of relationships among processes for constructing oral and written texts. Text is viewed as constructed in

31

action, language is viewed as being in use (social action), and meaning is defined within context' (Floriani, 1993, p. 243).

While the nature and functions of talk and literacy in the classroom are similar to those in the 'outside' world, language in all its forms within the classroom has uses that relate to specific cultural practices associated with schooling. As Gee (1990) points out, schools engage in particular discourses. To be a teacher or a pupil in any school demands specific ways of using language, behaving, interacting, and adherence to sets of values and attitudes. The ways in which we read and write are essentially the social constructs of specific groups. Individuals, in turn, are enculturated into these literacy practices and their meanings.

Classrooms are therefore places where knowledge is constructed as specific interactions between participants occur as part of the teaching and learning process, and as teachers and students live out their daily lives. While schools and classes may share many specific behavioural (e.g. participant roles), organizational (e.g. grouping, teaching strategies) and resource (e.g. curricula, texts) characteristics, they are all unique social constructs which are reflective of the specific background of their students and teachers, as well as the texts that are acknowledged and valued in their classrooms.

Heras (1993, p. 276) suggests that all classrooms have a range of 'lived opportunities, possibilities, and constraints opened up ... (and dependent) on the configurations made possible by the institutional organization of the school and classroom *and* by the social and academic interactions within these institutional spaces'. Hence, knowledge is always related to the opportunities students have to engage and interact with each other.

Negotiation is an important part of classroom life. Fernie *et al.* (1993) argue that classroom life involves constant negotiation between participants. Each of these participants negotiates roles, rights, obligations, norms and expectations from different positions. Heap (1991) points out that a teacher and his/her students jointly construct the contexts in which they work, defining the content of their learning, and the situated roles and relationships and the definitions of what counts as knowledge.

This has been illustrated by Gutierrez (1993), who found, when studying the effects of writing process instruction on elementary- and secondary-aged Latino children, that differences across classrooms were characterized by particular participation structures. That is, the social hierarchies, discourse and interactional patterns and knowledge exchange systems varied from classroom to classroom. Furthermore, she found that the various patterns of social action, discourse and classroom activities formed 'scripts' which were of three main types.

The first was labelled *recitation* and was found in four out of nine classrooms. It was characterized by a large degree of teacher direction and limited opportunities for students to interact with and receive help from peers.

The second was labelled *responsive* and was found in three out of nine classrooms. While this script was still very much 'teacher managed' it allowed for far more relaxed activity boundaries and participation structures, with student responses being solicited and encouraged, and opportunities given for students to build on the responses of others.

The third type of script was labelled *responsive/collaborative*, and was observed in two classrooms. This type of script was characterized by a highly dynamic interactive learning context in which both the discourse and the knowledge were more frequently jointly constructed. In this type of classroom, the teacher more regularly acknowledged student contributions, and writing was seen 'not as a method, or a set of activities, but rather as a socially negotiated process of constructing oral and written texts, of interacting with others about texts, and of generating texts' (Gutierrez, 1993, p. 345). What was clear from Gutierrez's work was that these differences between classrooms lead to the construction of specific models of literacy, rather than a single unitary definition.

The teacher, as pointed out in Chapter 2, has a vital part to play in the construction of classroom discourse. Through their actions, teachers signal what they see as appropriate actions, what roles are possible (and are valued), how students are to take up roles, and what count as appropriate literacy activities in the classroom (Heap, 1980).

Having said all of the above, I need to ask, why is it important? What does it mean for classroom teachers? I want to suggest the following implications:

- This work shows that the way teachers structure classrooms has a strong influence on the forms of literacy that are valued.

- It shows that the way classroom language is controlled and directed by the teacher ultimately makes a difference to the way students interact with and construct texts.
- It shows that the forms of spoken language that are valued and privileged in classrooms by the teacher have a direct relationship to students' patterns and possibilities for learning.
- The knowledge that students can gain is related closely to the opportunities students have to engage and interact with each other.
- The various patterns of social action, discourse and classroom activities sanctioned by the teacher and members of the class lead to the formation of specific 'scripts' (or frameworks) which inevitably place limits on the type of knowledge and literacy constructed and used in the classroom.

This issue is dealt with again in Chapter 4, and the roles of teachers and students examined in more detail.

'Apprenticeships' in thinking, language and literacy

As mentioned at the beginning of this chapter, one strong influence on my work has been the work of writers and researchers who have examined the relationship of language (and of course literacy) to education. A second significant influence has been the work of Vygotsky (1978) and the development of this work by Rogoff (1990).

Rogoff (1990) uses the metaphor of 'apprenticeship' to describe how children learn. She suggests that children are apprentices in thinking:

> ...active in their efforts to learn from observing and participating with peers and more skilled members of their society, developing skills to handle culturally defined problems with available tools, and building from these givens to construct new solutions within the context of sociocultural activity. (p. 7)

Rogoff's work in turn is based on the work of a number of psychologists whose theories are socially based (e.g. Vygotsky, Luria, Cole and Scribner, and Wertsch). Central to her concept of being apprenticed in thinking is the work of Vygotsky.

Vygotsky's (1978) theoretical work has two central concepts. First, that human activity has a tool-like structure, and second, that it is embedded in a system of human relations. Vygotsky argued that these two major features defined the nature of human psychological processes. His theory suggests that higher order processes like literacy can only be acquired through interaction with others, which at some later stage will begin to be carried out independently.

Central to Vygotsky's assumption that learning moves from an initial form of guided learning to later independent learning is his concept of the Zone of Proximal Development. Vygotsky's (1978) ideas challenge traditional notions of developmentally appropriate learning. He proposed that there are in fact two developmental levels. The first he termed 'actual development', and defined it as 'the level of development of a child's mental functions...determined by independent problem solving' (p. 86) – in other words, what a child can do alone at a particular point in time. The second, 'potential development', was defined as that which a child can achieve if given the benefit of support during the task. It is the ability to solve problems 'under adult guidance or in collaboration with more capable peers' (p. 86).

Vygotsky suggested that there is always a difference between these two forms of development and that this gap, the 'Zone of Proximal Development' (ZPD), indicates the functions 'that have not yet matured but are in the process of maturation' (p. 86). It is the ZPD that is critical for learning and instruction. He argued that learning creates the ZPD; it 'awakens a variety of internal development processes that are able to operate only when the child is interacting with people in his environment and in cooperation with his peers. Once these processes are internalized, they become part of the child's independent developmental achievement' (p. 90).

Rogoff (1990) points out that the ZPD is a dynamic region of sensitivity to learning the skills of culture, in which children develop through participation in problem solving with more experienced members of a group. Cole (1985) in turn argues that within the ZPD culture and cognition create each other.

Vygotsky suggested that teaching geared to developmental levels that have already been achieved will be ineffective, and that 'the only "good learning" is that in advance of development' (p. 89).

But how is this learning fostered, and what is our role in it as teachers? Bruner (1983, 1986) devised the concept of 'scaffolding' to explain this process. In explaining 'scaffolding' Bruner described the behaviour of a tutor helping 3- and 5-year-old children to build a pyramid out of interlocking wooden blocks. Bruner concluded that the act of scaffolding as observed was a process whereby the teacher helped students by doing what the child could not do at first, and allowing students to slowly take over parts of the text construction process as they were able to do so. The teacher controlled the focus of attention, demonstrated the task, segmented the task and so on.

However, some (e.g. Harste *et al.* 1984) have criticized the way Bruner defines this concept, suggesting that it places too much control in the hands of the teacher, who is seen as a manipulator and simplifier of the learning environment, attempting to reduce language learning to a series of stimulus-response bonds.

While agreeing with these criticisms, I am opposed to definitions that reduce the teacher's role to that of a passive manipulator of the environment. This stance implies that students will 'discover' all there is to know by being 'immersed' in learning. Such a viewpoint reduces the role of the teacher to that of participant with identical knowledge and status (something which is incorrect) within the classroom, and ignores the important functions that teachers need to perform as part of teaching (something which will be explored in greater detail in Chapter 4).

While I oppose the notion that teachers or peers should control the joint construction of someone else's text, Bruner's emphasis upon control may reflect the fact that he was reporting observations of an adult engaged in the construction of a pyramid. This may explain the extent to which the adult assumed control. The construction of a model provides an opportunity for another person to assume joint ownership for the task. I would argue strongly that the same potential does not exist when talking about texts created by language users. While two people may help each other to construct a text, each must ultimately make his/her own text, not simply create one that can be shared.

Within this book the term scaffolding is assumed to describe the behaviour of any person or persons which is designed to help a student engage in some aspect of learning beyond his or her 'actual' level of development.

It would seem that Vygotsky's (1978) work offers us more than a view of learning which restricts the teacher's role to that of one who simply prods or prompts students to mimic the behaviour or meanings of another person. As Rogoff (1990) reminds us, cognition and thinking are 'broadly' problem solving, and this in turn requires an active process of exploring, solving and remembering, rather than simply acquiring memories, precepts and skills. And problem solving reflects human goals that involve other people.

Rogoff's concept of *guided participation* is also useful to help explain how Vygotsky's views on learning can be put into practice in classrooms. This concept suggests that

> both guidance and participation in culturally valued activities are essential to children's apprenticeship in thinking. Guidance may be tacit or explicit, and participation may vary in the extent to which children or caregivers are responsible for its arrangement. (1990, p. 8)

In Rogoff's opinion, guided participation involves children and others in a collaborative process of 'building bridges' from children's present understanding and skills in order to reach new understandings and skills. This in turn requires 'the arranging and structuring of children's participation in activities' (1990, p. 8).

The relationship of Rogoff's concept of guided participation to Vygostky's work should be obvious. Central to guided participation is Vygotsky's concept of *intersubjectivity*. This is the process humans engage in when collaborating. It involves a sharing of focus and purpose between a child and another more skilled or knowledgeable person. This is essentially a process that involves cognitive, social and emotional exchange between participants in learning.

Of critical importance within this book is the way these concepts are applied in classrooms. It is obvious that some teaching styles would not encourage the development of intersubjectivity, nor would they in any way demonstrate Rogoff's notion of guided participation. For example, the various teaching scripts identified by Gutierrez (1993) which were discussed earlier in this chapter would seem to offer different potential for guided participation to occur and for intersubjectivity to develop.

Teachers who employ *recitation* scripts and who provide only limited opportunities for students to interact with and receive help from peers would no doubt reduce dramatically the opportunities for guided participation to occur.

It would seem that Vygotsky's concept of the Zone of Proximal Development, and Rogoff's concept of guided participation, have great relevance to teachers who are concerned with helping students to acquire literacy. What Rogoff's work contributes is an emphasis on the active participation of learners in their own development. As Rogoff (1990) points out:

> Children seek, structure, and even demand the assistance of those around them in learning how to solve problems of all kinds. They actively observe social activities, participating as they can. (p. 16)

There is a complementary process involved where the teacher and peers help as the student attempts to learn beyond his or her actual level of development. The role of other participants in this learning may involve the provision of new knowledge or strategies, but this should normally be in response to the student's attempts to learn. That is, the teacher or other students should not be the ones who constantly set the learning agenda; rather, they should respond to the learner's needs as he/she grapples with learning within his/her Zone of Proximal Development.

The teacher or peers assisting the learner may offer new knowledge or demonstrate strategies, but, as Rogoff points out (1990), this need not be explicit or even didactic instruction, something which is in contrast to that stressed by Vygotsky (1978) and Bruner (1983). Rather, while it may be explicit, it may also be indirect and at times non-verbal. Rogoff suggests that there need not be intentionality in communication between learners and their peers or the teacher. In fact, she suggests that most of children's lives in many (if not all) cultures involve interactions that are 'organized to accomplish the task of the moment' (1990, p. 18).

The only qualifying comment I would want to add to Rogoff's argument is that while this may well be true of the home and community, particularly for the young child, the world of schooling is characterized by a far higher level of explicit and didactic instruction than most educators would see as desirable.

In a nationally funded research project that aims to describe the literacy practices of the final year of primary school and the first year of secondary school, Cairney *et al.* (1995) have found that a large proportion of classroom time is devoted to teacher talk of a didactic kind. While this is not to suggest that Rogoff's argument is incorrect, it would suggest that in many classrooms, teachers are adopting teaching styles that are far more consistent with Gutierrez's (1993) *recitation* script, which is characterized by a large amount of teacher direction and limited opportunities for interaction. Less evident were *responsive/collaborative* scripts, which are associated with the creation of a more dynamic interactive learning context. This in part relates to the way teachers use questioning. This will be discussed in greater detail in the next section of this chapter.

Teachers are more than simply manipulators and trainers. The interactions between parents and their young children are frequently cited (e.g. Snow, 1983; Painter, 1986) as the ideal models for learning. It is worth remembering that what is central to these interactions is a shared history, love, trust and concern for the child's right to construct his/her own meanings. As Bruner points out (1986, p. 132), we need to enter into dialogue with a learner in such a way that 'hints and props' are provided to move him/her through the Zone of Proximal Development. Learning is not about detached teachers taking control of learning away from students; it is about support, help and encouragement to reach new levels of understanding and skill.

The work of Vygotsky and Rogoff obviously has a number of implications for the teacher:

- Instruction and curriculum should be directed at a level just beyond the child's current level of development.
- The teacher should construct learning environments which permit students to attempt tasks with the help and support of the teacher and other learners – that is, create contexts for guided participation.
- Teachers have an important responsibility to observe the learning of students to determine their actual and potential levels of development, and to identify their Zones of Proximal Development.
- Teachers must create learning environments which provide positive demonstrations of literacy. Students need to observe other readers and writers using literacy in ways that are beyond the student's level of actual development.
- Teachers should create classroom contexts which permit the teacher as well as peers to build bridges between class members' present understanding to new understanding and skills.
- Classroom environments should be places which permit intersubjectivity to develop. Such contexts are probably best described as communities of learners, like that created by Susan Langbien (see Chapter 2).

- Teachers must beware of the tendency to always make decisions about what is significant for learners within their classrooms. When teachers take total control of learning away from students, guided participation gives way to a new form of direct instruction. Bruner (1986) alludes to this issue when he asks:

> Is the Zone of Proximal Development always a blessing? May it not be the source of human vulnerability to persuasion…is higher ground better ground? Whose higher ground? (p. 148)

Questioning and the teacher

Questioning has long been recognized as an essential tool of the teacher. The teacher of literacy has always made extensive use of questioning as an instructional technique. However, frequently its use for reading instruction has been to test knowledge or simply interrogate texts. Tierney and Cunningham (1984) suggest that when it is used only in this way questioning does little more than test ability to extract information from texts and contribute little to student learning.

Nevertheless, questions are important tools for the facilitation of literacy learning. This has been confirmed from studies of language interactions between adults and children in the pre-school years, and comprehension research. Research on spoken language has indicated that adults constantly use questions to facilitate meaning making (Bruner, 1983; Snow, 1983; Painter, 1986; Wells, 1986). Also, comprehension research indicates that questions have great potential as facilitators of meaning making (Tierney and Cunningham, 1984).

Questions obviously have an important role to play in guided participation. For the teacher, this will mean asking questions, answering student questions, and encouraging students to ask questions of each other.

Questioning as a tool for learning has its roots in Socratic teaching. In the modern era of schooling it has a central place. The use of the question dominates textbooks, tests, teaching manuals and curriculum documents concerned with literacy. Teaching and questioning are seen as almost synonymous. Hyman (1979) suggests that to think of teaching without questioning is impossible. Teachers almost habitually ask questions, presumably to stimulate student thinking and test understanding.

A number of researchers have examined the volume and quality of questions asked by teachers (e.g. Stevens, 1912; Moyer, 1965; Flanders, 1970), and conclude that questions occupy up to 80 per cent of school instructional time, that these questions are primarily directed from the teacher to the child, and that they are frequently closed, simply seeking a single answer. In one interesting study, Hoetker and Ahlbrand (1969) found that teachers asked on average around two to four questions per minute.

Stevens's (1912) study was one of the first which described teachers' questioning behaviours. Since then a large number of studies have been conducted relating primarily to practice, rather than theories of questioning (Dillon, 1982). This research has described the teacher's use of questions (frequency, rate and type), the success of training teachers in using a range of questions, and the effectiveness of specific questioning techniques (e.g. the type of question, who delivers the question, and when the question is asked).

In spite of the large volume of research into questioning, Dillon (1982) has expressed doubts about its validity, suggesting that it has been concerned typically with practice, rather than theory development. He suggests also that there are puzzling contradictions between the use teachers make of questions and the use made of them by non-teachers. For example, he points out that many professionals (e.g. doctors) ask questions because they do not know the answer, and assume that the person to whom the question is addressed might. Teachers, on the other hand, frequently believe that they know the answer, and ask the question because they believe the student also needs to know. However, since the student does not ask the question, he/she may have no desire to know what the teacher knows anyway, nor might the student have any need of the knowledge.

Dillon questions whether such an approach to questioning can serve the purposes of enquiry. Therapists, he suggests, are warned not to ask too many questions because they restrict interaction. Teachers, on the other hand, appear to ask many questions assuming that they will stimulate and encourage enquiry. Teachers use questions as a predominant technique, whereas other practitioners avoid them. Such contradictions are not only confusing, they cast doubt upon the suggestions that are being made to teachers about questioning (Cairney, 1990b).

A major concern of reading research has been the development of taxonomies of questions (e.g. Barrett, 1976; Pearson and Johnson, 1978) influenced directly by Bloom's (1956) Taxonomy of Educational Objectives. Implicit within these taxonomies is the belief that the amount and kind of thinking varies in relationship to the type of questions that have been asked. Taxonomies like Smith's (1970), which identified four major question types – Literal, Interpretive, Critical and Creative – have been used widely, and have been useful for heightening teacher awareness of the need to move beyond recall of factual details (see Cairney, 1983/1990 for a fuller discussion). However, research concerning the role questions play in reading suggests that the relationship between thinking and the questions asked is not as simple as originally thought.

Cairney (1990b) suggests that one of the major problems with taxonomies is that they invariably consider questions in isolation from the reader, the text and the context. Many factors appear to influence the effectiveness of questions. For example: Who formulates and asks the questions (teacher, trusted adult, peer, the learner)? What is the content of the question? At what stage in the learning cycle is the question asked (before, during or after the task)? Within what context is the question asked (a formal lesson, group sharing, class sharing)? The application of taxonomies without regard for these factors may well explain why the effectiveness of questions has been shown to vary quite dramatically from one study to another.

It appears that teachers assume there is a direct and positive relationship between the type, frequency, rate and timing of teacher questions and the learning of their students. Research evidence, however, has provided rather mixed and at times contradictory results. In spite of this, most teachers, researchers and educators would agree with the assertion of DeGarmo (1911, cited in Wilen, 1982) that 'to question well is to teach well'. One of the problems, of course, is that teachers do not always question well. In fact, even curriculum materials designed to help teachers to question well have been shown at times to present poor models for questioning. Beck et al. (1979), for example, found that within basal reading manuals the questions asked were more random than coherent, frequently focused on trivial details, and were of little help to readers constructing a coherent understanding of the story.

In an interesting study of the use of questions, Wiesendanger and Wollenberg (1978) raised doubts about their usefulness. While able to cite a number of studies (e.g. McGaw and Grotelueschen, 1972) that have shown that asking questions before a passage is read facilitates comprehension, the researchers identified other studies which indicated that the opposite was the case (e.g. Markle and Capie, 1976). In relation to post-questions the results were more predictable, but still inconsistent. Anderson and Biddle (1975) found that post-questions had a facilitative effect in 37 out of 40 studies when the students were tested on the same post-questions. However, when new questions were introduced the effects were only moderate, and appeared in only 26 of the studies.

Interestingly, other studies have suggested that the type of question asked has an influence on the effectiveness of post-questions. For example, Rickards and Hatcher (1976) found that questions based on text content of high structural importance facilitated learning from texts to a far greater extent than those based on content of low structural importance. Similarly, Denner (1982, cited in Tierney and Cunningham, 1984) found that 'higher-level' questions produced a greater effect upon learning than 'lower-level' questions.

On the other hand, research evidence concerning the use of questions during reading indicates more positive effects. For example, studies conducted using a wide range of readers, texts and instructional contexts (e.g. Rothkopf, 1966, 1972; Graves and Clark, 1981) have shown that students given the opportunity to respond to inserted factual questions as they read perform better on the same questions when they are given as a post-test. Nevertheless, there is a lack of evidence concerning the effectiveness of questions used with a variety of text types and in a range of 'real life' learning contexts (Cairney, 1990b).

While interest in questions used during reading has been strong, there has been less systematic study of questioning associated with writing. However, Graves and Giacobbe (1984) suggest that, traditionally, questioning in writing lessons has been rather didactic, with the teacher asking children questions to which they believe the children know the answer. However, the shift towards 'process writing' in the early 1980s saw an associated shift in the nature of questioning in writing classrooms. Implicit within the methodology of process proponents like Graves (1984) and Walshe (1981) was a changed perspective on questioning. Questioning was seen as a tool to allow the teacher to discover what the student knew about the text they were writing and a means of encouraging them to reflect on their own text prior to revision. This perspective is seen in the work of Graves and Giacobbe (1984), who suggest that teachers of writing should ask questions about writing to gather information about child growth, and to contribute significantly to the growth of children themselves. Questions, they argued, should not be designed so much to test knowledge and transform it to that of the teacher, but rather to encourage students to explore their own understanding and potential. This is in stark contrast to much of the work on the role of questioning in reading. The exception, of course, is the more recent use of questioning in relation to reader-response-based approaches to literature (this will be discussed in more detail in Chapter 5).

Giacobbe (cited in Graves and Giacobbe, 1994) used questions as the basis of an instructional study of a group of 23 6-year-old children. She created a writing environment within her classroom that permitted children to write every day about topics the children defined, and in which opportunities were given for students to share their writing with each other in a variety of structured and unstructured ways, including group conferences and conferences with the teacher. The basis of Giacobbe's instructional work with the children was a standard set of six questions which were asked before and after the children wrote. Each of these questions was broad and open and was designed to elicit information from the children for the benefit of the teacher, and also to enable students to work towards more effective and clear meaning in their writing. For example:

How are you going to put that down on paper? (before)

How did you go about choosing your subject (for writing)? (before)

What are you going to do next with this piece of writing? (after)

What do you think of this piece of writing? (after)

While these questions were generic in nature they were designed to be supplemented by other questions that would elicit other information. Over the six months that Giacobbe conducted her study the

questions were modified and supplemented when additional information was required of the writer. Eventually, three major categories
shaped the questions they asked, information, process and standards.

Giacobbe's students made significant progress throughout the
study and she concluded that the questions had been an important
part of the success of what she had done. Her work showed how
questions could be used in a different way from the traditional
teacher use of didactic questioning. Giacobbe emphasized that questions should be used to find out how children change and learn. The
challenge, she suggests, is then to make sense of the information the
children give when responding to their questions. Teachers, she
suggested, should look for the following:

> The child's use of detail, ability to talk about the subject, sense of option,
> tentativeness of judgment, [and] growing language to talk about the
> process of writing.

While Giacobbe used a number of quite generic questions, some
process-based writing advocates have suggested more specific focused
questions designed to direct student attention on the meaning or
accuracy of their text (e.g. Cairney, 1981; Walshe, 1981). Such questions are often modelled by the teacher but are ultimately designed
to be used by students to talk about other student writing, or for self-
reflection on writing as an aid to the revision process. For example:

What do you mean by that sentence?

Is there a better way to start that sentence?

How could you make the meaning of that sentence clearer?

Is that the correct spelling of ...?

Interestingly, the use of open questions of this type and the type used
by Giacobbe has been criticized in recent times. For example, Christie
(1990) has claimed that this approach discourages teachers from intervening in children's language learning, particularly writing, and that it
creates an unnecessary distinction between process and product.
While there is an element of truth in the claim that some process writing advocates did discourage teachers from intervening, this was not
the intention of process writing philosophy as developed by Graves
(1983). What arguments like Christie's fail to recognize is that the

process writing movement was, in part, a reaction to the predominantly didactic approach to the teaching of writing that had dominated Australian classrooms in the 1960s and 1970s, and which had done little to develop children's written abilities. Process writing was an attempt to move away from teacher-directed approaches to learning that left little place for the student's voice to be heard or for students to take control of their learning. Questioning was seen by these advocates as offering potential for the development of self-questioning and reflectivity in students, and greater commitment to their own learning.

There seem strong grounds for greater emphasis on self-questioning, especially given the dominance in most classrooms of teacher questions. A number of researchers and educators have claimed that we should devote more attention to student questions (Carner, 1963; Gall, 1970; Dillon, 1982; Tierney and Cunningham, 1984) because of their apparent low incidence. For example, Floyd (1960, cited in Gall, 1970) found that students contributed less than 5 per cent of the total number of questions asked in grades 1–3. And yet student questions are thought to play a significant role in learning (Dillon, 1982). Related to this interest is the role that self-questioning can play in comprehension development. While few studies have investigated this, there is evidence to suggest that it has a positive effect on learning. In particular, the work of Palincsar and Brown (1983) has found that students trained in self-questioning show gains in reading.

In conclusion, there is little doubt that questioning is a major tool used by teachers to facilitate learning. However, the research in this area is conflicting and confusing. While there is clear evidence for the usefulness of questions it seems that the influence upon learning varies, depending upon (a) the type of question asked, (b) the timing of the question, (c) the text type being read, (d) the way in which the question is asked, and (e) the teacher's purpose in asking the question (Cairney, 1990b).

What needs to be stressed is that the role that questioning plays in the classroom cannot be separated from the way classroom learning environments are constructed and the curriculum defined. The work of researchers like Gutierrez (1993) shows that the various patterns of social action, discourse and classroom activities within classrooms form specific 'scripts' which dictate how teachers act and how students are invited to participate in their own learning. Questioning is just part of classroom discourse, and its use is shaped according to the scripts that teachers define within their classroom.

Back to the teacher, the student and the text?

What should be obvious from the above discussion is that there is a close relationship between talk and literacy. Moreover, teachers have a vital role to play in student growth and development. This occurs explicitly through the instruction they give and the way they offer information, question or just talk about texts and learning, and implicitly, through their demonstrations of literacy and learning, the things they value, and the way the learning environment is constructed in classrooms.

The concepts of scaffolding and guided participation already introduced in this chapter are obviously of critical importance to any discussion concerning the teacher's role in student learning.

As Rogoff (1990) has pointed out, adults influence children's learning by providing access to and regulating the difficulty of tasks, but also by structuring children's involvement in learning situations through joint participation. The essence of teaching is the creation of 'supported situations' in which children extend current skills and knowledge.

The concept of scaffolding is of critical relevance here. As described earlier in this chapter, the term scaffolding is used to describe the behaviour of any person(s) designed to help a student engage in some aspect of learning beyond his or her 'actual' level of development. This definition implies a number of key principles:

- Scaffolding is not simply something employed by teachers or adults – it can involve peers who possess greater knowledge or skill in specific situations.
- Scaffolding is more than simply prodding or prompting students to mimic the behaviour or meanings of another person – it requires the student to be pushed 'beyond him/herself'.
- Scaffolding is a response to student attempts at learning. Others engage in guided participation with the student as he/she attempts to move within the Zone of Proximal Development to new understandings or skills. This help may involve the provision of new knowledge or strategies, but primarily this occurs in response to the student's attempts to learn. That is, the teacher or

other students do not make decisions before learning takes place concerning the help needed; rather, they respond to the learner's needs as he/she grapples with learning within a specific ZPD.

- Students take responsibility for their own learning, they create their own texts. Those providing scaffolding support simply help them to arrive at the meanings they have initiated – they do not take responsibility away from them.
- As Bruner points out (1986, p.132), scaffolding involves entering into dialogue with a learner in such a way that 'hints and props' are provided to move him/her through the ZPD.

Wood, Bruner and Ross (cited in Rogoff, 1990, pp. 93–4) describe six functions that are typically associated with scaffolding for the teacher (or tutor, or fellow student):

- Recruiting the child's interest in the task as it is defined by the teacher.
- Reducing the number of steps involved in the solution of the problem by simplifying the task.
- Maintaining the pursuit of the goal, through motivation of the child and direction of the activity.
- Noting inconsistencies between what the child has produced and the ideal solution or outcome.
- Controlling frustration and risk during problem solving.
- Demonstrating an idealized version of the act or skill to be performed.

What is worth noting from these functions is that the teacher provides both a clear structure for learning and support of a variety of kinds. The functions can be easily transformed into terms that relate to literacy.

In summary, this chapter has tried to stress the vital relationship between talking, listening, reading and writing. Teachers have a vital role in recognizing and building on this natural relationship which has a critical influence on learning.

Broadly, teachers need to:

- create classroom learning environments that recognize the close relationship between talking, listening, reading and writing.
- create learning contexts that permit students to be 'apprenticed' into literacy learning.

- talk to students and question them about language, literacy and learning in such a way that they are supported as meaning makers and develop as reflective learners.

In Chapter 4 I will explore how these ideas can be translated into effective environments that help students to become more effective readers.

CHAPTER 4
Creating literacy environments

In the previous chapter I spent a great deal of time discussing the complex relationship between language, teaching and learning, the way in which students are 'apprenticed' into ways of thinking and using language and literacy, the role that questioning plays in student learning, and, finally, the way teachers scaffold literacy learning in the classroom. What should have been apparent from the discussion is the close relationship between classroom talk and literacy learning, and the way in which we as teachers socially construct specific learning environments. When these are viewed alongside the arguments developed in Chapter 2 concerning the sociocultural nature of literacy, we begin to form a picture of the type of environments that I want to recommend we should attempt to develop in our classrooms. So often in classrooms, the curriculum that students experience seems to be based on the joint premises that literacy is simply a cognitive process and that the teacher's role is to impart skills to aid that process. As a result, individual learning and achievement is encouraged and collaborative learning is viewed suspiciously. While there is tremendous variation in the ways teachers create literacy learning environments, I want to suggest that the things we believe about literacy and learning will have a major impact on the way we create literacy learning environments in our classrooms.

As Table 4.1 attempts to illustrate, there is a close relationship between one's assumptions about literacy and learning and one's classroom practices. For example, the way teachers view the manner in which meaning is made will affect one's teaching. Views on this topic vary between two extremes. The first group includes teachers who believe that meaning is derived as the reader or writer utilizes a range of essential sub-skills that are used in a sequential way. At the other end of the continuum are those who see reading and writing as constructive processes that are very much meaning-driven.

While Table 4.1 is somewhat dichotomous, I accept that the world of teaching and learning is not as simple as this. For example, it is

Table 4.1 The relationship between assumptions about literacy and learning and teaching practices

	Implicit with this book	*Alternative*
EXAMPLE 1	Reading and writing are both constructive processes that require a reader or writer to make meaning	While writing requires composing, reading is seen as a process of meaning extraction. Both are seen largely as linear skills-based processes
Implications for practice	Programmes are created that stress the importance of meaning	Programmes stress the teaching of decontextualized sub-skills
EXAMPLE 2	Readers and writers are seen as active participants in the creation of texts	Readers and writers are seen as passive consumers (or copiers) of other people's meanings or text forms
Implications for practice	Readers and writers are encouraged to take greater control of their literacy learning, choosing texts, purposes and genres that are appropriate to their learning needs	Readers and writers have little choice in literacy learning, with texts, genres and purposes being largely determined for them
EXAMPLE 3	The teacher's role is to support literacy learners as they try to make meaning, questioning, providing information, and offering assistance as needed	The teacher's role is to determine the students' skill needs and teach them in a systematic and largely sequential way with the skills work often an end in itself
Implications for practice	Teachers attempt to provide scaffolding support so that students work to their potential level of development	Teachers attempt to provide sequential skills development often with much repetition and with a presumed common hierarchy in mind for all children
EXAMPLE 4	Literacy learning is seen as a social process	Literacy learning is seen largely as a psychological process
Implications for practice	Collaboration is valued and students are encouraged to work together, sharing understanding and supporting each other	Individual learning and attainment is valued; personal goals, skill development and competition are stressed at all times

accepted that literacy is both an individual and psychological process as well as a social process. However, the purpose of the table is to give some sense of how quite different assumptions about literacy learning will lead to different teaching strategies. For this reason it is important for me to outline some of the key assumptions that underpin all that is said in this book. I want to address these assumptions in three main areas, those concerned with the role of the teacher, those concerned with the role of the student, and those concerned with literacy.

What is the teacher's role in this type of classroom?

While it is obvious that the teacher is one of the most vital elements in the classroom, the positioning of the teacher has a large effect on the type of literacy practices that are encouraged in classrooms. For many teachers, their role is very much on centre stage. If their classroom was a play, they would concurrently fill the key roles of director, producer and lead actor. They set all agendas, ask most of the questions, determine who says what to whom and for what purpose, and then end up talking and performing most of the time anyway.

This type of teacher chooses the texts, sets the learning activities (which are often prescriptive with little choice being offered), and decides what the meaning is that students should acquire as part of the reading process, or what they should create in their writing. In short, all power and control is in the hands of the teacher. As Freire and Macedo (1987) and Giroux (1983) have pointed out, this is hardly the right way to go about empowering individuals. Graves (1983) has also stressed that if we want to develop students who are committed to learning, who delight in the experiences they share within school, then we need to show them how they can take control of their own learning.

In classrooms dominated by teacher-centred skills-based practices we find students who:

- rarely choose books to read for purposes which they see as legitimate
- rarely write for purposes which they see as real and significant
- are required to read books and materials which are unlike reading matter in the 'real world'

- are required to complete writing assignments which are frequently unlike any in the real world (either in purpose or form)
- are given few opportunities to share their discoveries about literacy
- are not encouraged to share their responses to reading and writing with other members of their class
- fail to discover that reading and writing have many useful functions in the real world.

It should not be surprising to find that children who only ever experience reading and writing as something they do at school fail to see that it is an important part of their worlds. For these students, reading and writing are viewed as activities to which they must submit, and books as something containing words to be consumed (Cairney, 1987a). Reading and writing are rarely seen as something to be enjoyed and used for learning. Traditional school practices, like the use of basal reading programmes, have indirectly taught children they read so the teacher can either test them, or provide an activity afterwards. For many of these children reading and writing have only ever been experienced as school subjects.

They have been:

- given in neatly timetabled timeslots
- taught in ability groups
- experienced frequently as a boring and frustrating round class or group oral reading exercises
- based on reading material and writing topics which lack interest and variety.

Some children reach the end of the first three years of schooling with little more to look back on than a literate past featuring high points of characterization such as Pam, Sam and Digger (or other alternatives like Dick and Jane) and an assortment of story plots concerning dressing for school, lost hats, and trips to the fire station, airport and zoo.

If we want to empower our students as learners we need to provide a rich and stimulating body of sensory experiences to enrich their thinking. And since language is a tool of thought, this thinking will be fostered through a rich language programme. It seems that children learn best when they have a relationship with other people who not only expect them to learn, but actively encourage and support them as learners (Cairney, 1987a; Cairney and Langbien, 1989). Our role includes the following functions:

- Providing information that our students do not have is an important function for teachers. However, the role should not be one of filling assumed 'empty vessels'. The teacher needs to provide information when needed as a natural part of the learning process, as students seek to solve problems, gain new understandings or respond to various learning experiences.
- Listening to our students as they share personal discoveries about learning is also critical. Teachers need to provide many opportunities for students to talk, while we listen. In fact, teachers will be unable to fulfil other roles if they do not first listen to students to discover what they know and perhaps need to find out.
- Suggesting strategies that other successful readers use. If the students' current strategies are not working teachers need to be able to suggest others that might be employed.
- Sharing insights, successes, problems, pain and joy experienced in reading and writing. It is important for teachers to show that they are readers and writers themselves, and that they share some of the same delights and problems that students experience.
- Supporting students when their best efforts are not up to their normal standards. For example, if students fail to revise their work for publication then the teacher must fulfil the important role of supporter or coach. This is not simply a negative correction role, but rather should involve the teacher acting as a critical reader who is helping students to achieve their publication purposes better.
- Introducing new language forms, new authors, new uses for reading, alternative writing styles, new language, new writing topics, new purposes for writing and new audiences. One of the major mistakes of the 'process writing' movement in Australia was that in seeking to give greater control to students, teachers forgot that they have an important role to play in 'stretching' students beyond their present level of competence. This should not involve introducing lessons on aspects of language in a decontextualized way, but rather, a sensitivity to the needs of students as they attempt to make meaning in a variety of meaningful contexts. This role

requires a high level of structure and organization (see Atwell, 1987).

- Demonstrating real and purposeful reading and writing. Teachers must do more than talk about reading and writing: they must show students that both are an important part of their worlds. Teachers need to be enthusiastic members of the 'literacy club' (see Smith, 1988).

What is the student's role in this type of classroom?

The instructional approaches outlined in this book are strongly influenced by interactive learning theories. Students are not simply a reflection of a genetic blueprint or specific set of environmental dictates.

While the influence of heredity on learning is accepted, learning is not simply the unfolding of innately prescribed traits, nor the summation of infinite stimulus response bonds conditioned from birth. Rather, learning results when mismatches or conflicts occur between what the learner knows and the environmental stimuli (i.e. when a problem has to be solved).

As I have argued in Chapter 3, learning is facilitated when students are pursuing problems of significance to them or when they are attempting to master skills of importance when solving these problems. I have also argued that Vygotsky's (1978) concept of the Zone of Proximal Development is of great relevance when understanding how learning occurs. Learning moves from an initial form of guided learning with other more skilled learners to later more independent learning. Vygotsky's ideas have challenged traditional notions of developmentally appropriate learning.

Learning optimally occurs as students are supported to take risks, attempt new things, and explore new knowledge within their Zones of Proximal Development. As Vygotsky expressed it, 'the only "good learning" is that in advance of development' (1978, p. 89).

As I have also pointed out in the previous chapter, Rogoff's (1990) concept of *guided participation* is also helpful in explaining how students learn. Guided participation involves children and others in a collaborative process of 'building bridges' from children's present understanding and skills in order to reach new understandings and skills. Central to guided participation is Vygotsky's concept of *intersubjectivity*. This is the process humans engage in when collaborating. It involves a sharing of focus and purpose between a child and another more skilled or knowledgeable person. This is essentially a process that involves cognitive, social and emotional exchange between participants in learning.

If learning occurs as children attempt to solve problems then teachers have a responsibility to provide an environment which fosters problem solving. Furthermore, since learning is believed to occur as the child explores his/her world, opportunities need to be provided for this to occur. Children learn because of natural curiosity. Children learn best from first-hand experience, by doing things, by being involved in the process. Teachers need to create environments where this is possible. This requires the development of communities of readers and writers (Cairney, 1987a, 1987b; Cairney and Langbien, 1989) which value reading and writing. Learning is, after all, a social as well as a cognitive process. We learn from others as we engage in the process with them.

Learning also requires engagement. Students must want to learn; they must be intrinsically motivated. No amount of extrinsic rewards will help to turn students into lifetime learners. A starting point for engagement to occur is for students to be given control over their learning. We need to allow students to make many of the decisions necessary as part of learning for themselves.

The type of classroom environment advocated within this book assumes that students learn best when they:

- See the purpose for learning and understand its relevance to their lives in and outside of school.
- Feel free to take risks. Students need to be prepared to attempt the reading and writing of new genres. As writers they need to write for varied purposes and audiences, and as readers they need to experience a variety of purposes for reading and written genres.
- Experience varied and frequent reading and writing opportunities, and have many varied encounters with text.
- Learn as an extension of varied and meaningful social relationships. Reading and writing are social phenomena. Both are learned as an extension of relationships with other people (Cairney, 1987a). Accordingly, students learn best when they are given the opportunity to learn as part of social groups.

- Communicate their insights to others. Language is an important vehicle for learning. Students should be given frequent opportunities to share their meaning making with others.
- Experience success. While competitiveness can foster learning for some students in some limited situations, generally students should not be pressured to compete with each other. Rather, they should be encouraged to set personal goals and follow purposes that are of significance to them.

Lessons from the classroom

You will recall that at the end of Chapter 1 I stressed that for far too long we have been too concerned about literacy teaching methods, and not concerned enough about the environments in which all children have the optimum chance to acquire the literacy practices that will enable them to lead fulfilled and successful lives. I suggested that the central question that drives my practice is: what do I need to do to empower students to use literacy for ends which they see as relevant and legitimate? I want to suggest in this chapter that the simple (but far from complete) answer to this question is that we need to create classroom literacy environments in which students can be supported as they use literacy for a range of meaningful purposes. I want to provide an insight into the characteristics of classroom environments that enable this to occur by sharing a number of classroom vignettes, which Harste *et al.* (1984) call 'literacy lessons'.

A SPONTANEOUS RESPONSE

The first literacy lesson is from a grade 1 classroom in which I was working as a collaborative researcher. I had been in this classroom observing the way the books a teacher reads often find their way into student writing (see Cairney, 1990c and 1992a for a more detailed description). This process of interpreting one text by means of a previously read or composed text has been labelled 'intertextuality' (see Chapter 2 for a fuller discussion).

As I explained in Chapter 2, the term intertextuality is in a sense a metaphor used to describe the constant construction and reconstruction of meaning, as readers and writers 'transpose texts into other texts, absorb one text into another, and build a mosaic of intersecting texts' (Hartman, 1990, p. 2).

Reading and writing occur against a backdrop of one's prior literary experiences. Most readers if probed will indicate that they frequently think of other books as they read. Similarly, many writers freely admit that the germs of their writing can often be traced to previous literary experiences with texts written and read (Cairney, 1990b, 1990c, 1992a).

One of my first observations as I entered the grade 1 classroom was that intertextuality was being shaped as students read and wrote together, and as an extension of their relationships with the teacher, and each other. The links between texts experienced were occurring within rich networks of relationships, with the texts playing a key role in social relationships. Sometimes the response of one child would lead naturally to the response of others. One example of this occurred after I had read the well-known book *The Jolly Postman* (Ahlberg and Ahlberg, 1986). After finishing the book I allowed time for students to chat about it, then sent them back to continue with a range of language activities (including writing).

Within ten minutes, one student returned to show me a letter that she had written which was obviously inspired by the book we had just read (Figure 4.1). She announced:

> Look Mr Cairney, I've written my own Jolly Postman letter. Chlorissa is writing one too.

Within twenty minutes there were at least ten letters in preparation, and by recess the whole class was writing 'Jolly Postman' letters. It was then that I was confronted by a small group of students (holding their letters) who politely demanded:

> Mr Cairney, we'll have to write our own Jolly Postman book. Could we do one?

Within a few days the class had produced its own version of the Jolly Postman book with the teacher's help. This literacy lesson illustrates how classroom environments provide the opportunity for students to build textual histories as they relate to others and share experiences of reading writing. This shared textual experience is a vital part of the creation of a classroom environment in which students can learn from each other, and in which they can feel free to share their personal reading and writing experiences. It illustrates also how students read and write as extensions of the relationships they share

Dear Gi+n

I am sorry i took your hpar. Hen

and gold. I cood nr help it.

They used to belog

to my dad But I am still sorry for

tarlcing them. Love from Jack P.S.

I will gro a anathev bin stalk

Figure 4.1 Sample letter produced by a grade 1 student in response to the book *The Jolly Postman*

with other students and, as a result, how their reading and writing is influenced by the reading and writing of others.

This second literacy lesson concerns a discussion that took place with a grade 5 class that I had been teaching weekly as part of a professional development activity in a New South Wales school (Cairney, 1990a). The discussion concerned part of Heide's (1975) book *The Shrinking of Treehorn*. This book tells the story of a boy who wakes one day to find he is shrinking. He continually appeals to his parents, but they take little notice. I read the story up to a point where Treehorn heads off to the den in disgust, then suggested to the class that they break into groups to discuss what would be some of the strengths and weaknesses of shrinking.

After approximately ten minutes the groups reported back to the whole class. The diversity of responses provide an interesting insight into the things that specific students valued, and the different personal histories into which they were assimilating this text (Figure 4.2).

What is interesting about this example is that it also illustrates how classrooms can be constructed in such a way that students are given the opportunity to share understandings of texts, and in the process jointly construct new meanings. This occurs as students listen to the responses of others, and in the process gain an insight into the meanings that others derive, the intertextual connections that are made, and aspects of texts with which other students engage.

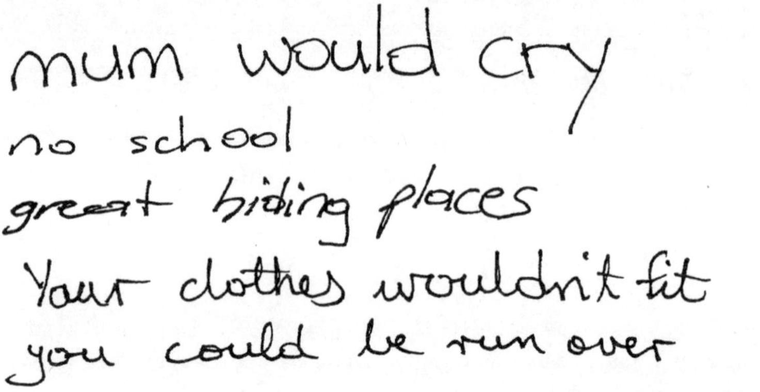

mum would cry
no school
great hiding places
Your clothes wouldn't fit
you could be run over
heaps cool —stir the teachers
sneek under doors
couldn't reach
the table
my brother would love it
birds would be a hazard.
watch out for cars
Yuk! I'd hate it !

Figure 4.2 Shared responses from a grade 5 classroom to a discussion concerning the consequences of shrinking

USING DIALOGUE JOURNALS IN GRADE 5

During 1990 I spent considerable time observing the work of a grade 5 teacher. One of the literacy strategies that the teacher was using to stimulate her students' literacy development was dialogue journals.

Dialogue journals provide an opportunity for students to write each day about things which are of interest to them. However, the audience for this type of journal is not simply self. The teacher is also an important audience and actually responds within the journal to the student's daily writing.

The teacher allowed her class to write for approximately fifteen minutes each day and then took the journals home each evening so that she could respond. Her responses varied in length from a sentence to half a page, and included answers to questions, jokes, new information, personal insights, personal information, questions and so on. They took her approximately thirty minutes each day to complete.

Within weeks of introducing the dialogue journals it was possible to observe:

- a strong commitment to this writing
- a growing knowledge by the teacher and students of each other as people
- an increase in the length of texts
- increased familiarity with the audience
- parallel improvement in writing in other areas.

One child (Troy) had refused to write virtually anything before the dialogue journal was introduced. In fact, for the first three weeks of their use, he wrote only token entries. But suddenly, one day his teacher responded in a slightly different way. In her response, she questioned him about the topic which was clearly his greatest passion – Scouting.

The response to this piece, and part of the next entry that follows it, gives some idea of the degree of intimacy between the two parties in the dialogue journal (Figure 4.3).

Within days the entries became longer, the topics more varied, the degree of intimacy significantly deeper, and the interest in writing greater.

The question might well be asked of the example in Figure 4.3 – why did Troy suddenly show new interest in and commitment to his

Troy, I loved reading your journal. I learnt so much about cubs. I never realised that they did so many interesting things. When I was a Brownie (many, many years ago) I can only remember doing things like sewing- never was much good at it! I learnt the semophore but I think I've forgotten it now..

allrite I wont menshen whote my sister duds at Bronvies then Mis Canny Well Bownding is my seck end best sudgeked cubs is my furist best sudgeked Daniel is a derker eck to the wnafom at muskied on the 26th of March 1990 Daniel wore his cubs skusks to skool at musked he musked up A thars a cubs suk ue how indarising Miss Canny isent it adorstle potsetive indrasira totle indrast

Figure 4.3 Sample extract from Troy's journal

writing? I think the answer is relatively simple. He saw the writing in which he was engaged as personally relevant, but more importantly, on this occasion, he could see that his teacher was interested in what he had to say.

This literacy lesson illustrates how important it is for students to see the reading and writing undertaken as personally significant. Also, it once again illustrates the important role that relationships play in the classroom (Cairney, 1987a). In an effective literacy learning environment teachers value their students, and attempt to build strong personal relationships with them.

REFLECTING ON CHARACTERS FROM *THE PINBALLS*

The fourth literacy lesson (see Cairney, 1990a for additional details) occurred within a year 4 class in which I was working to provide enrichment in the area of language. I had been reading *The Pinballs* (Byars, 1977).

This book concerns three abused and neglected children who find themselves thrown together with an ageing couple who have spent a lifetime rearing a total of seventeen foster children.

The story revolves largely around the relationship between the four central characters: Mrs Mason, Carlie (a street-wise kid with all the answers), Thomas J. (a timid boy brought up by ageing twin sisters) and Harvey (who is immobilized because of two broken legs).

After reading five chapters of the book I stopped and invited the class to consider the central characters and compare them on a range of human characteristics. I suggested the first characteristic to them (kindness/unkindness), and then used character rating scales (see Johnson and Louis, 1985; Cairney, 1990a, 1990b) to direct discussion. Essentially, this strategy requires students to draw a simple continuum with a specific characteristic and its opposite trait written at opposite ends of the scale. Students place characters on the scale in a position which reflects their rating of each on that specific trait.

The class broke into groups of three or four students and was encouraged to rate each character (Figure 4.4). Each group attempted to reach consensus. Approximately five minutes later the groups were invited to share their responses with the whole class. As they did so I attempted to construct a rating scale on the board which represented the class consensus.

At all times during this lesson it was stressed to the students that there was no single correct rating. They were encouraged to share their perceptions and to provide their reasons for rating the characters the way they did. This process was repeated for a further two character-istics – confidence/timidity and intelligence/lack of intelligence.

An interesting postscript to this lesson was that approximately one week later, near the end of the reading of this book, I asked them to repeat their rating of the characters. I then shared with them the results of their earlier deliberations. To the group's surprise, the rating for the character Carlie had changed dramatically on two characteristics rated previously.

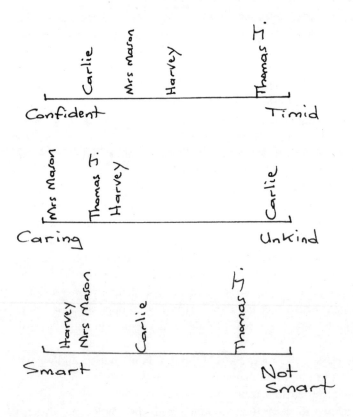

Figure 4.4 A grade 4 class response to the use of rating scales with *The Pinballs*

One of the interesting things about this example is that response provided both an insight into student constructions of specific characters and, at the same time, an opportunity for them to reflect upon each character and negotiate these meanings with other readers.

This process, and the experience of reading the book itself, ultimately saw them change their views quite dramatically concerning the central character. Initially, Carlie was seen as a confident but nasty person who lacked intelligence. By the end of the book, most students had decided that she was now a confident, intelligent and kind person. Presumably, they had looked beyond the superficiality of this character's gruff manner, and decided that deep down she was an insightful, gentle and loving person.

One of the main things that this literacy lesson illustrates is the teacher's important role as an initiator of talk about text, and a catalyst for revisiting texts. The literacy teacher should not be someone who simply provides books for children to read. The teacher must constantly encourage students to talk about text in order to learn more about language and their world.

WRITING IN SCIENCE

This literacy lesson is borrowed from Judy Turner, a former colleague, with whom I worked for a number of years while employed as a language consultant. Judy was teaching a 2nd/3rd grade composite class at the time, and was using an experience-based integrated curriculum. One of her integrated programmes during the year involved the class rearing eight chickens. The class fed, played with, observed, drew, and investigated these chickens for a period of three months.

One of the strategies Judy used in her classroom was a journal in which children wrote daily. Figure 4.5 contains two pieces of writing (and illustrations) that one student produced three weeks apart following observations of the chickens.

What do we learn from this literacy lesson? Quite simply, we witness the power of personal experience. Literacy teachers need to recognize that students need to be given the opportunity to make sense of their world. They need to be given the opportunity to use reading and writing as vehicles for learning. In this example, writing was used to record their observations and then reflect upon the things they have observed. This in turn provided an opportunity to revisit the meanings they had created in order to construct new meanings and hence to use language to learn about their world. The second text and its illustrations show just how much this child had learned as he had observed the chickens and used language to explore his growing understanding.

CHANDA FINDS HER OWN PURPOSES FOR LANGUAGE

In the mid-1980s I spent six months teaching a grade 5 class in Indianapolis (USA). I was in the classroom involved in collaborative research with Jean, a teacher in her first year of teaching (see Cairney, 1987b for a more detailed description). Jean had asked me

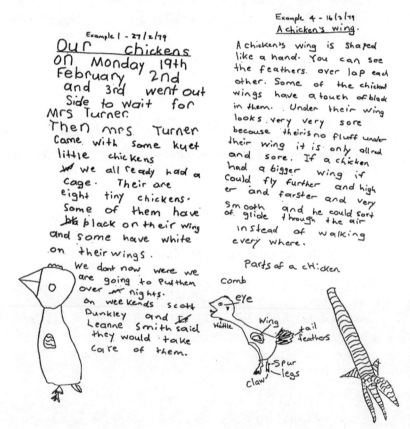

Example 1 - 27/2/79

Our chickens
on Monday 19th February 2nd and 3rd went out Side to wait for Mrs Turner.
Then mrs. Turner Came. with some kuet little chickens we all ready had a cage. Their are eight tiny chickens. Some of them have black on their wing and some have white on their wings.
We dont now were we are going to put them over nights.
on weekends scott Dunkley and I Leanne Smith said they would take Care of them.

Example 4 - 16/2/79
A chicken's wing.

A chicken's wing is shaped like a hand. You can see the feathers. over lap each other. Some of the chickens wings have a touch of black in them. Under their wing looks very very sore becouse their is no fluff under their wing it is only all red and sore. If a chicken had a bigger wing it could fly further and higher and farster and very smooth and he could sort of glide though the air instead of walking every where.

Parts of a cHicken

comb
eye
wattle
Wing
tail feathers
spur
legs
claw

Figure 4.5 Two entries from one grade 2 child's science journal showing observation of chickens

to work alongside her to implement (in her words) a 'whole language' classroom. It was in this classroom that I met Chanda.

Chanda was an African American from the inner city, who came to the school on a bus each day as part of the city programme to integrate minorities into 'mainstream' schools. She had little interest in schoolwork and spent most of her day being disruptive and attempting to avoid work. It was almost impossible to get her to write.

However, one day I noticed her typing something before school began. She reluctantly allowed me to read her piece (Figure 4.6).

LONESOME. ALL ALONE WAITS FOR THE PHONE.

LONESOME ALL ALONE WAITS FOR A CALL BUT

BUT THERES KNOW CALL AT ALL.

LONESOME ALL ALONE.

LONESOME ALL ALONE WAITS FOR A SOUND

BUT ALL SHE COULDEE HEAR IS A FADING

EOUND.

LONESOME ALL ALONE WANTS TO PLAY BUT ALL

IT IS A GLOOMY RAINY DAY.

LONESOME ALL ALONE?   WHAT CAN SEE DO

LONESOME ALL ALONE WANTS TO PLAY WITH

YOU.

BY CHANDA

Figure 4.6 A musical text written by Chanda

I talked with Chanda about her piece and discovered that she had a desk full of similar pieces that she had been composing for some time. It appeared that Chanda had a passion for rock music which she shared with her brothers and friends. As we talked about her interest she told me that she spent most of her weekends wandering the streets with a ghetto blaster on her shoulder.

This literacy lesson taught Jean and me something valuable about literacy. While we had set up a classroom environment designed to provide opportunities for students to engage in literacy practices that we valued, Chanda had resisted our literacy. However, at the same time she was actively engaged in other literacy practices which she saw as more relevant to her world. This literacy lesson illustrates the importance of classroom environments being created in such a way that students are able to use literacy practices that they see as valuable. As teachers we have to provide opportunities for students to bring their everyday texts into the classroom where they can be recognized and supported and built upon.

What do these literacy lessons illustrate collectively?

The examples chosen have been fairly arbitrary selections. I could have shared hundreds, based on as many texts, written and read by children of all ages. However, I'd like to suggest that while each of the above examples has illustrated a number of significant individual points, collectively they illustrate what I see as the essential features of classroom environments that empower students to use literacy for ends which they see as relevant and legitimate. I want to summarize the essential features under three subheadings: classroom interaction; the teacher's role; and characteristics of the literacy programme.

CLASSROOM INTERACTION

I believe that the examples I have shown illustrate some distinctive features of the classroom interaction that was fostered:

- The focus of the group or class interactions was upon making meaning as a text was encountered or written – not on activities. This is important. Classrooms where activities are the focus, rather than meaning making, are characterized by set topics, limited ranges of options for reading and writing, and repetitive use of particular activities (e.g. oral reading and completing worksheets).

- When group activities were initiated by the teacher, all members were given an opportunity to contribute. Indeed every voice was heard at some stage in the lessons from which the literacy lessons were derived. This contrasts quite starkly with classrooms where few children are given a chance to respond, where more able or dominant students take over discussion, and where the focus is on individual work.

- Students shared their meanings and often explained how they believed they had reached this understanding. This contrasts with classrooms where students keep opinions to themselves, or where the focus of discussion is upon guessing what is in the teacher's head.

- The interactions were open exchanges. That is, there was no assumption on anyone's part that there was only one meaning. This is an important element of exciting literacy environments. While it is not meant to imply that any interpretation of a text is a relevant one, or that conventions and form are not important to writing, such an environment encourages risk taking rather than rewarding narrowness of thought.

- Students used (and at times were encouraged to use) a variety of modes to express and share their meanings. This is critical. While this book is concerned primarily with reading and writing, it needs to be remembered that there are other ways of making meaning including viewing, drawing, drama, sculpture, computer design work and craft.

- The teacher challenged students to relate the texts to their own world. One of the keys to the teaching of reading and writing is to engage readers and writers with texts. This can only be achieved when readers are able to relate the text to their pre-existing knowledge, their prior textual experiences and their personal interests, and writers feel deep commitment to what they are writing about.

- Meaning was negotiated and personal texts often reshaped in the light of shared understanding. Such environments do not seek to develop students who simply produce texts which conform to socially defined values and ideas. Rather, they seek to open students' eyes to other potential meanings which they ultimately must consider and either assimilate or reject.

- Response acted as an important vehicle for reflection on the reader's growing understanding of a text that had been personally constructed. In other words, response provided a means to revisit a text that had been written or read. This recrafting of one's knowledge is an important element of learning.
- Meaning was often jointly constructed as students and the teacher responded to each other's meanings. This is an important aspect of interaction in classrooms like those described in the vignettes above. Interaction often occurs as students and the teacher negotiate meanings, jointly writing or interpreting texts.

THE TEACHER'S ROLE

It is obvious from the above discussion that teachers have a vital part to play in the type of classroom environments that are being advocated. It is often the teacher who ensures that talk about text is facilitated (or extended), and that key textual understandings are discussed.

However, the teacher should not be simply an interrogator of students and texts. He/she has to expend a great deal of energy trying to refrain from the tendency to tell the class what the text (or even the product of the student's response) means, or how a text should be written or rewritten. Students must first be given an opportunity to think for themselves. If the teacher offers advice too quickly, he/she may cut off opportunities for students to explore creatively other options for meaning. This is not to say that teachers do not have a role in sharing insights (the opposite has been said above), but rather to warn against teachers too quickly taking control, and in the process, reducing possibilities for student growth and learning.

An important part of this role for teachers is the use of questioning in a different way. As I pointed out in Chapter 3, classrooms are probably the only context within our world where someone asks a question to which they already know the answer. If we are to create exciting and challenging literacy learning environments, then questions need to be used in a different way. They need to be:

- Inductive as well as deductive. Deductive questions start from a set of given facts and attempt to lead students towards a specific answer. On the other hand, inductive questions encourage students to discover alternative explanations for something. The former directs the student's thinking in a set direction, while the latter elicits a reaction and encourages a search for multiple solutions.

- Open more often than closed. Open questions permit many answers while closed questions desire a single 'correct' answer.
- Asked by students as well as the teacher. Some classrooms only allow room for the teacher to ask questions. Our aim must be for students to ask questions of the teacher and each other.

However, while the teacher does not tell the students what the text means, he/she does not simply encourage the class to make a text mean anything they want it to be. Rather, he/she encourages students to consider the 'endless possibilities' that a text holds (Cairney, 1990c) as they build meaning which is textually and culturally appropriate.

CHARACTERISTICS OF THE LITERACY PROGRAMME

The above literacy lessons also reflect literacy programmes which have a number of distinctive characteristics. The following are of considerable importance.

- Social and cultural variation was recognized. In each of the classrooms from which the literacy lessons were derived, the teachers had developed programmes in which the social background and culture that the students brought with them to the classroom was not only recognized, but was foundational to much of what was done. This was shown in the choice of reading materials, the resources provided for classroom use, the way students were given opportunities to contribute, and the role that parents played in literacy (see Cairney and Munsie, 1992b). Programmes of this type not only recognize and value social and cultural variation, they encourage the development of genuine partnerships between the school and community (this will be discussed in greater detail in Chapter 9).
- Literacy was valued and broadly defined. A second important feature of literacy programmes in the classrooms from which the above vignettes were derived was that literacy was not defined narrowly as a school subject. Rather, the classroom practices reflected at least an implicit acceptance that literacy is a wide range of specific cultural practices which students have a right to access in accordance with personal needs and life goals.
- Meaning was central. The starting point for all of the literacy practices outlined above was a concern to construct meaning

which was relevant and important to the student him/herself. In each classroom, students were encouraged to take risks as they made meaning, not stay within parameters defined by the teacher. Hence, literacy activities were never set simply for the sake of completing a literacy task. Rather, opportunities to use literacy were provided so that learning could take place.

- Social interaction was central to the classroom practices. In each of the above classrooms, interactions between classroom members was encouraged, with frequent opportunities given for collaboration with other students and for group learning. In all classrooms we need to provide frequent opportunities for students to spontaneously share their insights and discoveries about language. In each of the above examples, the need to maintain social control was not the teacher's central concern. The need for social control should always be kept in perspective. No, we cannot allow our classes to 'run riot', but remember that any imposed restriction on language use has an impact upon its potential for meaning making.

- Students were 'pushed' beyond current learning. Each of the literacy lessons was also reflective of programmes in which students were given support as they encountered literacy. In each case they were helped to use literacy to make sense of their world; they were not simply taught about literacy. As I argued in Chapter 3, learning ideally occurs when we are stretched beyond our current potential.

- Purposes for literacy were self-defined. While there is always a place for teacher imposed reading and writing, in the above examples students were given the opportunity to pursue literacy for purposes which they saw as legitimate, interesting and engaging. When programmes are devised which allow students to control their own learning, rather than simply being coerced or persuaded into it, students display different attitudes to learning and ultimately superior outcomes.

Conclusion

The preceding discussion concerning how classroom contexts might be constructed is an attempt to describe the characteristics of learning environments which I believe provide the optimum potential for students to learn literacy and learn through literacy. It is clear that all teachers desire to see children learn and succeed in the wider world. What is needed in the 1990s is a response of some kind by all teachers to the inequalities of opportunity that surround us. If our classrooms are to be places where students are introduced to a range of literacy practices and where they are empowered to assume control of these practices, then we need to create classrooms in which there:

- is commitment to using reading and writing for personally relevant purposes
- are opportunities given for students to share their insights and discoveries as they make sense of their worlds
- are significant relationships that exist between teacher and students and among students
- is a recognition of a broad range of literacy practices
- is a personal excitement about learning and the place that literacy has in learning
- is a genuine attempt to respond to and be shaped by the cultures from which our students are drawn.

We need to avoid the tendency to adopt unitary definitions of literacy and in the process to impose a limited range of literacy practices as the yardsticks by which we measure success in schooling. We need to break down these limited perspectives of literacy.

As I outlined in Chapter 1, there is a twofold task ahead of us as teachers. We need to recognize the multiple literacies that are present in our society. At the same time we have a responsibility to introduce our students to a range of literacy practices. For many students the latter can only occur if they first discover that these alternative literacies can be personally liberating. I believe that these discoveries will only be made if we reshape the classrooms within which our students live and grow for thirteen years. This will involve continually reminding ourselves that our schools are part of society, and recognizing that they must reflect and serve it, rather than simply helping inadvertently to maintain existing inequalities. Part of this reshaping will involve teachers rethinking their role in student literacy development and use. An important part of this is the development of students who are avid readers. This important topic is the focus of Chapter 5.

Developing readers who read

While the field of literacy education is strewn with hundreds if not thousands of books and papers that have suggested new and 'revolutionary' methods to enhance literacy learning, I want to focus in this chapter on something that has always been fundamental to literacy success, that is, the development of a thirst for reading and the regular reading of texts. It was Frank Smith (1971) who coined the phrase 'you learn to read by reading'. While this statement seems simplistic to some, it is nonetheless true. One of the major tasks for teachers is to develop avid readers in their classrooms. This is obviously critical in the early years of schooling if children are to make rapid growth in written language development. If children can acquire a love of reading in the first years of schooling, and see its relevance for learning, it is almost certain that they will go on to become successful in all forms of literacy. However, it needs to be stressed that how this is acquired may well vary for particular children and even complete cultural groups.

Traditionally, one of the most common pathways to literacy has been through listening to and later reading literature. This is hardly surprising, since narrative is such a fundamental and central part of human existence. Literature has obvious benefits for the entry of children into the world of literacy, but increasingly teachers are beginning to question whether this is the only (or even optimal) pathway. Could some children more effectively be introduced to the world of literacy through the use of factual texts? What about technological text? Could we be entering an age when young children will be introduced to the world of reading through visual display terminals that parents use daily to order groceries, check the television programme, and communicate with friends and family? Perhaps! What about interactive video, the use of CD ROM technology, visual communication and so on? What role will they play in emergent literacy? I am unsure, but perhaps it will be significant. My personal view is that literature and the book (even if in electronic form) will continue to be major vehicles for children's entry into the world of literacy – certainly in most cultures. This issue will be discussed in greater detail in Chapter 9.

In this chapter, I want to start by exploring the use of literature in the classroom, describing classroom strategies that support readers as they read. However, I also want to explore other forms of reading as potential pathways to literacy.

Discovering literature – a personal history

It took eight years of my life before I read my first book, and yet I read it after being a 'reader' for four years! It was Jules Verne's *Twenty Thousand Leagues under the Sea*. Sure, I had read school readers and some school magazine stories, a few comics and one edition of *Boys' Own Annual*, but I'd never read a novel of my choice. In effect, I had learned to read but did not read regularly for other than school purposes.

I believe that *Twenty Thousand Leagues under the Sea* taught me things about reading that I'd never known before. I lived through this book (to use Rosenblatt's well-known phrase) – I could almost smell the leather in Captain Nemo's cabin. I felt the panic of the sailors on the wooden hulled ships as the terrifying sight of a glowing 'eyed' monster came hurtling towards them in the darkness. I felt compassion for the people inside doomed to death. There was a sense of excitement and commitment to the text evoked by this story that simply could not be generated from the reading of the school readers I had experienced as a child, each with a range of banal plots and impoverished language and characterization. I gave lots of myself to the text and engaged with the story and with its characters.

I believe this book changed me as a reader, turning me from a passive consumer of text into an active meaning maker. Not a consumer of words, but a creator of text! I read this book many times and in time others besides (with many twists and turnings along the way – but that's another story).

Years later I was to observe many children who, like me, as young children never read books except to complete a school task. They were delivered to my doorstep by concerned parents to enrol in a community literacy programme I had set up. I discovered something interesting. Virtually all the children who had reading problems behaved as if they were reading textbooks. These students, like myself as a child, were mere consumers of other people's texts, not creators of meaning in the fullest sense of the word. The attention of these readers was often focused on the surface features of the text, and not necessarily on the construction of meaning. Freebody and Luke (1992) have suggested that this focus on text features, while important, is but one role (the *code-breaker role*) that readers must assume. They argue that readers need also to engage with a text by inferring connections between textual elements and background knowledge (*text-participant role*); they need to learn how to respond to texts in social contexts discussing and relating texts to other texts (*text-user role*); and finally, they need to learn how to interrogate texts to consider the sociocultural factors which underlie the interpretation of the text (*text-analyst role*).

My own experience of reading and that of the many students with whom I have worked over the years has taught me that reading can be simply a school task for some students which moves little beyond Freebody and Luke's code-breaker role, or a vehicle for almost endless meaning making which moves readers into all four roles when encountering text.

As teachers our definitions of what literature is also has an effect on the way we value and use literature in classrooms. For example, some teachers see it as a vehicle for sustaining our cultural heritage. For those who see literature in this way, it is the means for ensuring that all students have access to an assumed central and essential cultural knowledge based on an exclusive canon of special literature. Other teachers see literature as the provider of significant experiences which are seen as central to the social fabric of family life. This 'warm fuzzy' (essentially middle-class) view of literature is often associated with images of curling up near the fire to read that special book.

While one cannot deny that there are elements within each of these definitions that have merit, each misses the point that literature must inevitably be seen as culturally generated and defined text – a living tapestry of yesterday, today and tomorrow. For example, those who suggest a cultural heritage argument in support of their approaches to literature assume that their cultural heritage is *the* cultural heritage that all students should have. This may be permissible in a monocultural society (if one still exists) but it is a problematical view in today's complex multicultural societies. Literate texts are written within a specific culture and reflect varied cultural perspectives. In turn, the way literature is valued, and even read, is culturally defined. Our aim should be to develop readers who are capable of analysing and critiquing the texts that they read, not simply readers who conform to the ideology of these texts.

Literature's potential

Literature offers many children their first opportunity for sustained reading experiences. Through the early story reading of parents or caregivers young children begin to develop concepts of print and related early print decoding skills. Parents read and point to print (and pictures of course); children run their fingers over the text mouthing words, inventing new ones, and generally engaging with the adult and the text to construct a unique telling of the story. From these beginnings children soon start to identify words, memorize texts and begin to explore story more fully. And all the time they are learning about language and their world, as well as continuing to build relationships with those who share these textual experiences.

As the child grows the literature becomes more complex in plot and genre, in language and content. They begin to be confronted and learn as they build an ever enlarging intertextual history. Hopefully, our readers also begin to move in and out of reader roles like those described by Freebody and Luke (1992). Our aim is for them to move from being simply readers who decode the texts to readers who use them for a variety of purposes, who can relate them to other texts that they have read, and who eventually can reflect on their meanings and purposes.

There are many who, locked within their narrow and limited conceptualizations of what literature is, fail to identify all that it can offer. Literature is not just about story, it is about life, and one's world. I want to suggest that literature can fulfil many complex functions. It can act as:

- a mirror to enable readers to reflect on life problems and circumstances
- a source of knowledge
- a source of ideological challenge

- a means to peer into the past, and the future
- a vehicle to other places
- a means to reflect on inner struggles
- an introduction to the realities of life and death
- a vehicle for the raising and discussion of social issues.

Most books offer the potential to address many of these functions at once. For example, *Charlotte's Web* (E. B. White) simultaneously offers new knowledge about spiders and the animal world, addresses the complex issue of dying, and deals with many elements of the human condition, including love and companionship. *Summer of My German Soldier* (B. Greene), on the other hand, provides an insight into life in the Second World War and the difficulties of those trapped in one culture while being linked to another. At the same time it raises numerous ideological issues for the reader to consider and address.

Literature offers 'endless possibilities' for readers to explore their world and learn from it, to enter 'other worlds' and to engage in meaning-making (Cairney, 1990a).

Creating rich literary environments – developing a sense of community

I believe that the starting point for introducing students to the world of literature is to look at the reading environments we create in our classrooms. The classroom environments we create are reflective of our assumptions about language and learning. One of the problems we face as teachers is that much of our knowledge is tacit. Each of us operates according to a set of inherent assumptions about literacy, learning and teaching (Hutchings, 1985). These assumptions direct our thinking as teachers, and influence the type of learning environments we create within our classrooms.

It took me a number of years to realize that literature can be a vital part of the common ground that I am able to share with the students in my classrooms. The turning point came in my second year of teaching while teaching a grade 6 class. I started the year as I had ended the previous one, using a primary school magazine containing extracts from literature and factual texts. I used this mainly for oral reading, comprehension activities (typically a set of 10 questions). I supplemented these lessons with a battered reading laboratory. Six weeks into the first term I was given a Core Library (Ashton Scholastic) by my school principal with the instruction, 'I want you to try this out'. The package was essentially a set of 100 children's books (mostly literature), some supporting materials designed to stimulate creative response to the texts, and a copy of Don Holdaway's (1972) book *Independence in Reading*. This book, and the Core Library itself, were to lead to changes that transformed my approach as a teacher.

I began to talk to my students about their reading, and in the process made many discoveries. I found that while they could all read (obviously to differing extents), none of them did, except for a range of school purposes. No one had read a book in recent times, and most had never read a complete novel. Even the best readers in this class could only recall one or two books they had read during the primary school years. The 100 paperback books provided the perfect basis for changes in my reading programme.

I began to make changes by introducing a daily independent reading programme. For thirty minutes every day I encouraged my students to read books of their choice. I also began to collect as many pieces of literature as possible to build up a class library. I arranged bulk loans from the school and community libraries, and asked children to bring in their favourite books. The class library was quickly established and my students began to read almost immediately. I introduced a system of conferences with my students (as suggested by Holdaway) which were designed to permit them to talk about their books. I also encouraged them to meet in groups to share their literary experiences. I began to provide time for my class to respond in their own way to the books they read. This response time utilized a variety of media and sign systems, including drawing, dramatization, writing, and craft. Finally, I began reading to them daily to share a variety of genres and authors' work. The results were overwhelming. By the end of the year this class had read over 1,500 books, with a range of 25 to 160 separate titles. All of these children were avid readers.

The change in my classroom was quite dramatic and went well beyond a simple change in my reading programme. At the beginning of the year my classroom was a place where:

- people worked quietly
- no one spoke unless spoken to

- tasks were usually completed alone, or on occasions, in ability groups with set requirements
- students completed only what was asked of them
- I marked set tasks and provided feedback in the form of scores, grades and, occasionally, written comments.

By the end of the year the classroom environment had undergone a number of fundamental changes. My classroom was now a place where:

- students talked to each other about their work and their interests
- activities were frequently completed in informal interest or friendship groups
- we frequently shared as a class our reading interests
- I talked with all students about their reading interests
- people recommended books to each other
- students frequently initiated literacy activities themselves
- students spontaneously responded to their reading in a variety of media, including drama, drawing, writing and discussion
- students began to analyse and reflect on the content, purpose and ideology of the texts we had been reading
- the students and I each responded to the work of others in a variety of ways including spoken comments, written responses (e.g. journal entries) and informal conversation.

What had happened in this classroom was that literature had provided a vehicle to transform a teacher dominated and teacher directed learning environment (Rogoff, 1994, refers to this as an 'adult-run' instructional model) to one based on the development of a community of learners. In this classroom both the teacher and the students were now active in managing and contributing to each other's learning. The students were now learning about literacy as they participated with each other in the exploration of literature. While much of the reading was being done silently and independently, students were constantly engaged in conversations about their reading, and were all contributing to the group's growing understanding of literature and their world.

This class had now become a community of readers that valued reading and gave it a prominent place in their lives. My students were no longer simply students who read because they had to: they now read because they wanted to. As the title of this chapter states, they were now 'readers who read'.

The classroom had now become a place where students:

- *Shared* personal discoveries, concerns, and issues that arose as they read literature
- *Reflected* on their discoveries, the insights of others, the texts they had been reading, group purposes and goals, and group priorities
- *Responded* to each other as people, as well as responding to each other's meanings, discoveries, problems and insights
- *Communicated* their discoveries, insights, feelings, values, reflections and purposes.

Furthermore, it had now become a place where the members of this community of learners provided positive demonstrations of reading and writing which had the effect of encouraging each other to:

- *Talk* about their reading
- *Construct* shared understandings of specific books
- *Critique* the texts that they had been reading and the views and interpretations of others concerning the text meaning and ideology
- *Read* independently for personal satisfaction and a variety of purposes.

Supporting readers as they encounter texts

One of the keys to the changes that I introduced as a teacher in my grade 6 classroom was that I adopted a new 'instructional model' (to once again use Rogoff's term). One of the key elements of this changed model was a change in my role as a teacher, from one who saw learning as the outcome of my teaching and the information I gave my students, to one who saw that my role was to structure a learning environment that enabled my students to more fully participate. My key role now became how to encourage my students to become more active managers of their own learning.

However, my role was not simply that of a silent passive observer. While I was an active participant, I also provided scaffolding support to all students. This support took many forms, but was consistent with the six functions outlined by Wood *et al.* (cited in Rogoff, 1990, pp. 93–4) and discussed in Chapter 2. Let me outline the form that this support took:

- *Raising interest in reading*
  This was achieved by:

  reading to my class each day to share my excitement about literature;
  forming discussion groups to allow students to talk with each other
      about their reading;
  encouraging them to share their reading with each other;
  providing opportunities for creative response to literature.

- *Simplifying the task of reading*
  This was achieved by:

  helping my students to select books at an appropriate level;
  introducing a variety of authors and genres in order to provide
      options for self-selection;
  reading some literature to them so that more difficult texts and
      authors were made accessible;
  providing a range of workshop strategies designed to focus reader
      attention on plot, characterization, and language (this will be
      discussed in more detail later).

- *Maintaining the pursuit of the goal*
  This was achieved by:

  meeting with each child each week in an individual conference to
      talk about the books they had read;
  keeping a record of all books read;
  praising students who had read regularly;
  making sure students were on task during reading sessions.

- *Noting inconsistencies in the children's reading*
  This was achieved by:

  reminding students that they needed to read regularly;
  encouraging students to keep a personal record of their reading;
  letting students know during individual conferences when their
      reading was less consistent and less varied than was desirable.

- *Controlling frustration and risk during problem solving*
  This was achieved by:

  creating a relaxed atmosphere that was not based on competition
      between students;

encouraging students to try new books, authors and genres even when uncertain;

answering student questions about books when confused by the language and the meaning;

developing a class climate in which students (as well as the teacher) could contribute to the maintenance of this supportive environment.

- *Demonstrating the act of reading*

This was achieved by:

reading to students every day in order to demonstrate the excitement of literature and language;

modelling questioning in groups so that students could replicate the approach when interacting with peers;

demonstrating that I read books regularly and that I enjoyed them; encouraging students to tell others about their reading as well.

A key to the effectiveness of the literature programme that was introduced was the nature of the interactions that I had with students. As Rogoff (1990) points out, all instructional models lead to learning; however, the approach that I had introduced in my classroom led to a different approach to questioning and talk about text. As I pointed out in Chapter 3, questioning is typically didactic and teacher-centred in many classrooms, something Rogoff points out is consistent with an 'adult-run' instructional model.

Instead of engaging in the rather didactic teacher-directed talk that characterizes many classrooms I began to talk about text in a different way. Rather than simply questioning students to see if they had constructed the meaning that I thought was 'in the text', I now began to use talk about text differently. I now supported readers as they worked at making meaning by:

- asking a variety of questions, many of which were open
- offering prompts to aid their understanding
- sharing personal insights about my reading
- giving information (context, author, concepts...) about texts when necessary
- listening to their responses to text and the meanings they had derived
- making comparisons between specific texts and other texts, experiences or ideas ('Do you remember...?' 'That's a bit like...')

83

- challenging them to read their texts closely and critically.

All the while I was helping my students to create more elaborate texts as they read and to make discoveries concerning:
- how literary texts work and are constructed (the text's genre, plot, characterization, setting, themes, style, literary devices and forms)
- the way texts intersect with their own lives (how did it affect them? what emotions did it evoke? did they like it?)
- the ways texts challenge their beliefs and understanding
- the ideology implicit within the text
- intertextuality (how did the text connect with other texts in their life including books, films and experiences?)
- what the text had taught them about their world and other people's worlds (did they learn about people, historical periods, the natural world, culture?)

One of the keys to this changed emphasis in my approach to the way texts were discussed in my classroom was, as mentioned above, my approach to questioning. Rather than closed questions that required a single answer, I began to ask more open questions that had many possible answers. The examples in Table 5.1 (adapted from Probst, 1988) provide an indication of the type of questions asked and the focus of each.

Response to literature

Response is a natural consequence of most reading events, irrespective of text genre or reader purpose. It is response which enables readers to share insights, seek clarification of meaning, offer new knowledge, etc. (Cairney, 1990a, 1990b). While it is important for all types of reading, it has special importance for the reading of literature. Response can be defined as

> any observable behaviour by a reader which follows and is directly related to a specific reading. Such responses can be either structured (and encouraged) by teachers, or unstructured and spontaneous. (Cairney, 1990a, p. 26)

Reader response can take many forms. It includes numerous spontaneous forms such as laughter, anger, frustration, a personal recommendation (e.g. 'Why don't you read this book about...?'), as well as

Table 5.1

Focus	Questions
A first reaction	What was your first reaction to this text? Explain it briefly. Why do you think you reacted that way?
Feelings	What feelings or emotions were you aware of while reading (or listening to) the text?
Plot	What were the major events of the text? What was the climax of the text?
Images	What images came to mind during the reading of the text? (Read it again.) Were the images the same the second time? How did they change? What new things were seen?
Associated memories	What memories did the text stimulate – people, places, events, sights, smells, feelings, attitudes…?
Textual elements	Were there any features in the text which caught your attention – words, phrases, images, devices, ideas…?
Judgements of importance	What is the most important aspect of the text for you?
Problems	Was there anything in the reading of the text that caused you problems (this might relate to content, language, form, etc.)?
Author	Do you have any feelings concerning the kind of person that the author is?
Involvement	Did you feel involved with this text or distant from it?
Other responses	How did your reading of the text (and response) differ from other group members? Did any difference really surprise you? Why?
Evolution of understanding	Did your understanding of the text change while you were reading it?
Evaluation	Did you like this text? Why or why not? Would you classify it as a good book? If so, why?
Literary associations	Did this text remind you of other literary works (poem, play, film, story, genre…)? What was the nature of the connection (e.g. image, word, event, personal experience, style)?
Ideology	Does the author appear to hold a particular point of view concerning…? What is his/her view? Why do you say this? Do you agree with it?

some which have been primed by the teacher. The latter might include dramatic responses, artistic responses, or simply a variety of written responses (e.g. character profiles, descriptions of the setting, etc.).

Irrespective of whether the response is spontaneous or planned there are obviously a variety of generic mental activities involved. Corcoran (in Corcoran and Evans, 1987) suggests four basic types of mental activity involved in aesthetic reading:

- Picturing and imaging – involves building up a mental picture, with the reader picturing the scenes of a book as if actually there.
- Anticipating and retrospecting – involves reader anticipating and hypothesizing about upcoming events, or reflecting upon the text they have been constructing.
- Engagement and construction – involves close identification with the text as the reader becomes emotionally involved in the text, identifying with characters and situations.
- Valuing and evaluating – involves readers making judgements about a text, which may require judgements about the worth of the text or simply their own value judgements concerning the events and situations that unfold.

While one might argue about the comprehensiveness of these categories they nevertheless provide a sense of the diversity of mental processes in which readers engage as part of response. The extent to which readers engage in each type will vary depending on the reader's degree of engagement with the text, breadth of related intertextual experiences, relevant prior experiences, reading purpose, immediate context within which the text is read, and, of course, ability to simply decode the print (Cairney, 1990b).

Response is obviously important to reading. In my 6th grade classroom, which I described above, it was part of the fabric that enabled a sense of community to develop and which allowed members of the group to jointly participate in each other's literacy learning. Response allows meanings to be made public so that others can evaluate them and react to them. Harding (1972) suggests that reading, like day-dreaming and gossiping, is a means to offer or be offered symbolic representations of life. These in turn allow us to reflect on the consequences and possibilities of the experiences we and others have. Just as I am affected by human tragedy in my world, I am also affected (although less intensely) by the tragedy of characters in books such as the sailors in *Twenty Thousand Leagues under the Sea*. By reflecting on these experiences we come to a greater understanding of ourselves and the world around us. Literature invites readers to 'share in an exploration, and extension and refinement of his [*sic*] and their common interests' (Harding, 1972, p. 224).

From the child's earliest beginnings with literature, this sharing is modelled by many parents and caregivers. While the way written text is introduced and used varies from one culture to another (as discussed in Chapters 1 and 2), the interaction with adults concerning text is an important foundation for later literacy development (this is discussed more fully later in this chapter). Wells (1986) found that adults who read to their children often encouraged them to relate their experience of the world to the story. He suggested that doing this may well be an effective way to help direct and control the processes of thinking and language. It seems that thinking and the development of a sense of story are closely related.

It would seem that there are many good reasons to encourage response. Cairney (1990a, 1990b) has summarized the reasons for encouraging response under the following headings:

● *Response is a natural consequence of reading and should never be suppressed.*
In Chapter 2 I argued that reading is a sociocultural activity, and hence is an extension of culture and social relationships. Response is a vehicle for the building of common ground with other participants with whom we want to interact and form relationships.

It needs to be stressed that not all responses are shared (some encounters with books are very private affairs), neither is it the teacher's role to attempt to force students to respond. Such misuse of response could well serve similarly to impose the ideology of the teacher upon the child. This must be avoided. However, in spite of this danger, response is an important ingredient for the development of a sense of literary community.

● *Reader response allows one to re-evaluate (relive) the experience of a text.*
As discussed in Chapter 1, reading is a highly constructive process of meaning making which requires the reader to constantly revise the text he/she is constructing in memory. Iser (1978, p. 67) describes reading as a dynamic process of self-correction which involves 'a feedback of effects and information throughout a sequence of changing

situational frames; smaller units constantly merge into bigger ones, so that meaning gathers meaning in a kind of snowballing process'.

That is, it is by reflecting on his or her responses to a text that a reader elaborates the meanings constructed. As we seek reactions from others we inevitably reflect on their interpretations, revising and reshaping our own personal texts.

● *Response is essential to help build common literary ground.*
Reading, as already indicated, is not learned or used (very often) in isolation, and hence it is regularly shared. Our shared understanding of literature is part of the common ground which shapes our thinking and behaviour. While those who hold a 'cultural heritage' view of literature would want to suggest a core of literature that all should have, this is not the point that is being made here. What I am suggesting is that relationships are typically built from a foundation of common ground, some basis upon which to interact with another person. While literature is not the only basis for common ground, it is a useful one and was obviously an important precondition for the changes that were made in the grade 6 classroom that was described earlier in this chapter.

● *Readers learn as a consequence of being party to the responses of other readers.*
A prerequisite for the type of changes in instructional models that Rogoff (1994) describes is the provision of frequent opportunities for students to interact with each other. While members of any group share common meanings because they share common values, experiences, knowledge and so on, their meanings are never exactly the same. The sharing of their reading experiences will inevitably lead to the expansion of one's understanding of text. Bleich (1978) describes literary interpretation as a 'communal act', a view that is rooted in the work of Bakhtin (1929/1973), who suggested language use is always subject to the operation of two distinct forces. The first (*centrifugal force*) leads to the production of diverse meanings as one draws on a unique store of knowledge, experiences, textual histories, etc. The second (*centripetal force*), which operates concurrently, reflects the tendency for the shared beliefs and experiences of a group to push it towards accepted socially constituted and preserved meanings. Encouraging the sharing of individual responses allows these communal

forces to operate freely, thus allowing class members to reflect on their meanings and hence reshape their interpretation of a text.

● *Response permits the teacher to make judgements and predictions about the students' reading processes.*

The responses of our students are laden with many potential insights about them as readers. Cairney (1990b) suggests that a great deal can be learned from students' responses to their reading whether spoken, drawn, written or dramatized. Every response is laden with information about the student's meaning making. Response enables all members of a class (including the teacher) to have access to the understandings that individuals are gaining; this in turn is an invaluable means to enable group members to support each other's growth and development as readers.

Other pathways to literacy

After spending so much time talking about the use of literature in the classroom it is important to return to the implied message of the title of this book, that is, that there are many 'pathways' to literacy. In Chapter 1 I discussed at length the literacy practices that dominate schooling.

But before any teacher can begin to discuss other pathways, he/she needs first to begin by reconsidering how they define literacy. If the teacher holds a very narrow view of literacy dominated by prose reading practices, then he/she will no doubt be hard pressed to find many pathways that do not include literature. And here we again face the dilemma discussed in Chapter 1. Is it sufficient simply to aim to introduce children to the narrow literacy practices that seem to dominate schooling in developed countries, or should one be seeking to introduce multiple literacies and hence begin to transform schooling? As indicated in Chapter 1, I believe that we have a responsibility to do both. It is important to provide children with the dominant literacy practices that are sanctioned by schools and wider society. However, we also have a responsibility to constantly recognize alternative literacies and hence provide alternative pathways.

When considering this issue it is also important to consider its two major dimensions. First, what other pathways are there for children to become literate? Second, what pathways are there to transform children who can read, but don't, into readers who can and do read for a range of purposes of significance to them? Essentially, the first issue deals with the written material used to introduce children to literacy, while the second is concerned with the instructional model that is employed in classrooms.

The use of literature as the entry point into literacy is a very middle-class practice, but as I have already indicated it is a practice closely aligned with social power. In societies where formal schooling is the norm for most children it is a very common entry point into literacy and one that is closely related to the literacy practices of the school. Nevertheless, in many cultures literature (particularly in written form) is rarely used at all. Such variations have implications for children's potential success in schooling.

Even in a developed country like the United States of America, Heath (1983) found tremendous variations in the use of specific literacy practices in three communities in the Piedmont Carolinas. Heath found variation in the acquisition of oral language, and the manner in which parents introduced children to literacy. Focusing on story reading she was able to document significant differences in community styles of literacy socialization.

Children in a white middle-class community (Maintown) were socialized into a life in which books and information gained from them was seen as having a significant role in learning. Parents and other adults interacted with children from six months using book reading events. They asked information questions about these books, and related the content to everyday situations, encouraging them to share their own stories. In contrast, children in a white working-class community (Roadville), while also being involved in book reading, had these encounters with text centred on alphabet and number books, real life stories, nursery rhymes and Bible stories. For these parents the focus was not on narrative, but on factual recounts of events. The parents asked factual questions about the books, but did not encourage the children to relate the books to events in their lives. In a third working-class African American community (Trackton), parents rarely provided book reading events. Instead, they used oral stories which focused mainly on fictional stories or placing familiar events in new contexts.

Each of these communities was inadvertently preparing its children in different ways for schooling. The children in Maintown performed well, whereas the children in Roadville did well in the early grades, but had difficulty after grade 3 as a greater emphasis was placed on analytic, predictive and evaluative questioning. The Trackton children were unsuccessful in school right from the start.

What was happening in each of these communities was that the place literacy enjoyed in their culture was helping to prepare these children, to greater and lesser extents, to succeed or fail in the school system.

But are there other alternatives? Can children be introduced to literacy through non-literate texts? The answer is yes. Collerson (1988), for example, provides an interesting insight into how his daughter acquired early literacy almost entirely from factual texts.

As Heath's research shows, some children already find their way into literacy through alternative pathways. For some children their first introduction to literacy is through environmental (largely procedural) texts. Parents read signs to or with their children, print on television is memorized and a variety of non-narrative books are objects of play and discussion. The Roadville parents' use of alphabet and number books is typical of how non-narrative texts can be used, although it must be noted that rarely are these texts used in total isolation from narrative texts.

The second, and in some ways more substantial question is to ask whether there are other ways to turn students from passive readers of texts to more active users of reading for purposes that are personally relevant and important. The key here seems to be: would it have been possible with my grade 6 class to substitute some other text genre, or purpose for reading, other than reading literature for enjoyment? Could another form of literacy have offered the same potential to lead to a changed 'instructional model' in my classroom? Could I have moved away from an 'adult-run' model to a 'community of learners' model without literature? The short answer is yes, although I would want to suggest that my suspicion is that literature is likely to be a more effective vehicle for many children due to the sheer dominance of 'story' in many (if not all) cultures.

The possibilities would seem to be numerous. The major alternatives would include a range of more factual genres, and perhaps electronically delivered text. In addition, I am sure that some would want to suggest that a more integrated approach to reading and writing might also achieve the same purpose. The following are just some of the ideas that would be possible:

- *An experience-based approach to science or social science.*
A class might be engaged in a major first-hand experience such as keeping and observing chickens from day-old chicks to maturity. They would observe them daily and record observations in a log book. They might keep records of their growth and development, their food intake, waste output, etc. They could draw the chickens and write about them, and of course they could seek out factual texts to learn new things to help inform their observations (the examples drawn from Judy Turner's classroom in Chapter 2 were part of just such a unit of study).

- *Newspapers as a vehicle to literacy.*
Newspapers offer great potential for transforming students as literacy learners. A class programme could be designed completely around the daily newspaper for a period of weeks or even months. Such a programme would engage students in the reading and analysis of newspapers as well as the writing of their own newspaper. A specific focus could be overlaid using a current news topic which could be followed (e.g. the war in Bosnia), or a particular theme (e.g. bias in reporting).

- *Technological approaches.*
One highly innovative way to break the cycle of passive use of literacy would be to engage children in literacy via personal computers. While a prerequisite for this approach would be consider-able resources, this is becoming more of a possibility in modern schools. This might work even better if two classes in separate schools (or even separate countries) agreed to embark on this technological literacy 'excursion' together. Using either the simple desire to communicate with each other, or a series of shared topics, the two classes could read and write electronically using computers, fax machines and electronic mail. The latter would of course provide the greatest potential for the students, making instant communication possible, and opening up access to numerous important databases.

- *The use of text sets.*

The final example is by the far the simplest and is dependent on access to a good supply of factual texts. In essence it involves the use of specific topics or themes to focus student learning. Like the literature-based approach described for my grade 6 class, it begins with the preparation of a class library. However, on this occasion the library of books is grouped around the topic or theme. While it may include novels, poetry and even plays, many of the books will be factual texts. The aim is to collect a variety of written genres which then act as a resource for students to explore the topic. This approach would provide fertile ground for intertextuality to operate across a range of genres. The way the books are used can vary greatly from approaches not dissimilar to the way I used the Core Library to the exploration of an integrated unit of study. However, even in the case of the latter, the programme would involve a lot of student collaboration, and the use of a variety of written genres.

In all of the above alternative pathways to the transformation of literacy in classrooms it is important to stress that it is not the type of text or even the activities undertaken with them that is critical. Rather, it is the instructional model within which they are embedded.

What is shared by each of these examples, and is common to the literature-based approach used in my classroom, is that a similar set of assumptions are driving each. These assumptions (as outlined in Chapter 4) are that:

- Reading and writing are both constructive processes that require the reader or writer to make meaning. Hence the programmes stress the importance of meaning.
- Readers and writers are seen as active participants in the creation of texts. Hence readers and writers are encouraged to take greater control of their literacy, choosing contexts, purposes and genres that are appropriate to their learning needs.
- The teacher's role is seen as being to support literacy learners as they try to make meaning, questioning, providing information and offering assistance as needed. Hence teachers attempt to provide scaffolding support within the students' Zones of Proximal Development.

- Literacy learning is seen as a social process as well as a psycho-linguistic process. Hence collaboration is valued and students are encouraged to work together, sharing, understanding and supporting each other.

What should also be noticed with all of these approaches is that reading and writing are frequently integrated. In the next chapter I look more fully at how teachers create classroom contexts in which writing is valued and fostered. While much has already been said about writing, Chapter 6 will focus specifically on how young writers are developed.

Developing writers who write

My central concern in this chapter is very similar to that of Chapter 5. In the same way that many readers can read but do not read for anything other than school purposes, many young writers fail to use writing for varied purposes that are related to their own agendas for learning. This reality was brought home to me while team teaching on a grade 5 class on the outskirts of Indianapolis in 1984. I had entered the classroom at the invitation of the teacher who was attempting to transform her literacy programme, from one centred on teacher directed learning and a reliance on textbooks to one which was more child-centred. The teacher was interested in Whole Language and had studied with Jerome Harste and Carolyn Burke at Indiana University. She commented: 'I want you to team teach with me and show me how to implement a whole language classroom.' While I would not have described myself as a whole language teacher, nor was I keen on 'showing her how to', I was nevertheless interested in child-centred process-focused curricula, and so readily agreed.

One of the things that became obvious to the teacher (Jean) and me once we began collaborating was that several students were not prepared to comply with simple requests to complete the school writing tasks (e.g. completing worksheets, questions from textbooks, copying notes from the board, completing basal reading activities, etc.) which had characterized this class up until then. One of these students was Chanda, whom I introduced in Chapter 3. As I explained in this previous chapter, she was a student who did everything she could to avoid school literacy. When it came to writing she simply found other things to do, and usually ended the lesson with nothing on her page.

The piece of music that appears in Chapter 3 was the first piece of extended text that I had observed Chanda writing. What became obvious was that while the literacy of schooling was not perceived as relevant to her own world, Chanda saw relevance in the literacy she defined and pursued herself.

In time I was to observe that each of the other students who had been reluctant to write in school were actively using writing and reading in their personal lives. As a result of these observations Jean and I capitalized on this student use of writing, legitimizing it and encouraging the students to bring it into the classroom. In this way their literacy was acknowledged and an avenue found for introducing them to an expanded range of literacy practices for personal use.

Creating the right environment for writing

One of the things that Graves (1983) taught us was that if we want children to become excited about writing we need to create writing workshops in our classrooms. If students only ever write when asked to, in a form that is prescribed, and to an audience that is principally the teacher (as examiner), then one should not be surprised to find there is limited commitment to writing, and that it does not have a central place in student self-directed learning. One of the critical lessons that we have learned from writers like Donald Murray (1982, 1984) is that writing is in fact a 'craft' and, as such, requires an appropriate environment in which the writer can explore this craft. Such an environment has physical and human elements.

PHYSICAL ELEMENTS

Writing is a demanding and at times frustrating task and as such requires the writer to feel comfortable in the writing environment. Just as a reader will search for a variety of places in which to read for different purposes, so too writers will seek out the most appropriate place to explore their craft. At times young writers will want to be in the library surrounded by reference books to aid their writing, while at other times their preference will be to sit under a tree scribbling notes. Some of us are lost without our computers, while others prefer to draft on paper.

While there can be no single ideal writing environment the following elements are important:

Class layout. Attempt to create a variety of spaces to write. For example, blocks of tables where students can write together, separate individual desks for more solitary work, special spaces away from

96

the classroom (verandahs or large corridors are ideal for this), computers within the classroom.

Writing materials. Provide a variety of paper (different sizes and colours, lined and unlined), writing books (e.g. journals for rough drafting) and writing implements (including computers, pens, biros, pencils and even crayons for younger writers).

Resources. Writers also need a variety of resources. These include access to a dictionary and thesaurus, spelling books (and spell checkers if using computers) and word banks. They also include access to an extensive class library of children's literature (a major source of inspiration for narrative writing) and a well stocked school library.

Published writing. Another important part of the writing classroom is the outlets used for publication. Writing classrooms should have evidence of the writing of their members. This serves to remind students that writing is often for publication and it offers a valuable resource for knowledge and ideas about writing. Writing can be presented as themed issues, individual titles bound like books, wall mounted prose, poetry or research work, or perhaps electronic publication for those who are using computers to network with other schools.

HUMAN ELEMENTS

As I argued in Chapter 1, literacy is very much a sociocultural as well as a psycholinguistic process. We rarely write completely alone, and we frequently share our writing with other people. We learn to write as we relate to other people. As a result, the relationships and interactions we permit (or don't permit) in our classrooms make a big difference to the type of writing environment that we create. The following elements need to be considered:

Interaction. It is important that writers have the opportunity to share their work or test their ideas out at the point of need. While there are often good reasons to restrict student movement around the classroom, we need to remember that this inevitably restricts the opportunities for students to interact with others and discuss their writing. Given the importance that such sharing has been shown to have in writing (e.g. by Graves, 1983; Murray, 1984), this is an important issue.

Audience. Closely related to the above point is the need for writers to understand the audience for whom they write. One of the early findings in writing process research (e.g. Martin *et al.*, 1976) was that frequently in classrooms children were writing for the teacher as examiner. Not surprisingly this reflected the way writing was planned, and the fact that it was largely assigned by the teacher, and then marked afterwards. What is needed, however, is the opportunity to explore writing for a varied range of 'real' audiences (Cairney, 1982).

Support. All writers need the support of other writers. In a classroom that has been developed around an instructional model based on the notion of community, this means that all members of the class have a role to play. While the teacher has an important support role to play, students also need to support each other. This will involve the use of writing conferences and informal feedback at the point of need. One of the keys in an effective writing classroom is for the teacher to model effective writer support strategies; this will involve demonstrating how to ask questions and how to comment on someone's work (more on this later in the chapter).

What are the essentials of a writing programme?

While the content of any writing programme will vary depending on the age of the students and their needs as writers, there are a number of essential principles (adapted from Atwell, 1987) which are vital for any programme.

- *Writers need time.*

It seems a truism to say writers need time – of course! But in essence the point to be made here is that writing is a craft that cannot be easily accomplished in neat timetable slots. In the same way that one cannot say 'Let's all finish reading the novel this period', we cannot expect writers to research, draft and revise their work in unison. It is important to allow writers the time necessary to explore ideas, talk to other writers, and revise their work. While there will always be specific classroom agendas that will place some restrictions on use of time (e.g. the need to finish a topic in science, the need to learn to write under exam conditions etc.), our aim should be to minimize these restrictions wherever possible.

- *Writers need to choose their own topics.*

It is also important for students to have some choice of writing topics. Whether they are involved in more creative narrative writing or writing in a range of factual genres across the curriculum, students will always show greater commitment to topics in which they have had some choice, compared to those that have been imposed. While it is important that students also learn to respond to imposed topics, teachers should provide student choice in writing topics whenever possible. Often this is relatively simple. For example, if exploring a major topic on the urban environment it would be possible to allow students choice of research topics (and hence writing topics) within broad topic headings. It is also desirable to allow students to choose written genres which they see as appropriate for such a topic.

- *Writers need readers to respond.*

Just as I argued in Chapter 5 that it is important for readers to hear the responses of other readers to texts they have read, as well as to revisit texts for further clarification of meaning, so too writers need the response of others to the texts they have composed. It is through the responses of others that writers test out their writing. It is by having others read one's texts that one discovers if the meaning is clear and if the purpose for writing the text has been achieved.

While all classroom members need to develop the ability to respond constructively to the writing of others, the teacher obviously has a critical role to play, both as an expert writer (with, presumably, greater knowledge of the writer's craft) and as a demonstrator of how one should respond to the writing of others.

- *Writers need to learn the writer's essential craft knowledge.*

Just as a potter or painter needs to learn the essential craft knowledge of his/her discipline, so too the writer needs to learn the essentials of writing. The writer needs to constantly build his/her knowledge of writing in four main areas:

Surface features. This refers to the essential mechanics of writing that enable one to be able to write in conventional forms. These include spelling, vocabulary, punctuation, grammar and usage.

Text knowledge. This refers to the more complex understanding of written register and genre. Writers also need to learn when to use a specific genre and written register for specific writing purposes and audiences (more on this later).

Resource skills. This refers to the writer's understanding of the many resource skills that all effective writers need. They include the use of dictionaries and reference material. Writers need to know how to find information when researching a topic, how to summarize or record this material for further use and how to retrieve information from libraries and computer databases for later use.

Wordprocessing skills. In the 1990s all writers also need to be able to use a wordprocessing programme including basic layout functions, spell checking, etc.

- *Writers need to see effective writing demonstrated.*

Once again, just as readers need to have teachers and other students who demonstrate effective reading, so too writers need to see effective writing and response to writing demonstrated. The teacher has an important responsibility to demonstrate writing for students and to read a variety of writing to the class to provide an insight into the range of written genres available. One of the advantages that writing has over reading is that there is much that can be demonstrated using an overhead projector or board. In a typical classroom students should be engaged in a number of related activities all of which contribute to their writing. These elements occur in no set order, but rather are part of a recursive cycle of related activities, all of which contribute to writing. They include:

Writing. This ideally will involve variable blocks of time in which students can write. Sometimes students need large blocks of time, while at other times they need the opportunity to write regularly when there are gaps in the day.

Preparation for writing. Writing usually requires some preparation. Sometimes this will simply involve quiet reflection; it may involve discussing the topic with a friend, a group, or the teacher; at other times it will require concentrated library research work or observation.

Talk about writing. As mentioned above, it is important at times to talk to others about writing. While this may occur as part of preparation for writing, it is also an important part of the ongoing writing process. Writers need regularly to share ideas, words, or even a whole text with other writers to gain a sense of their progress, or simply to celebrate a breakthrough.

Joint construction. At times it is useful to jointly construct a piece of writing with at least one other more skilled writer. Sometimes this will involve the teacher leading a lesson designed to result in a group (or even a whole class) jointly constructed text. This is particularly useful when introducing a new written genre. It may also occur in small groups with a specific student assuming leadership for the writing.

Revision. This is also an important part of the writing process. In fact, some writers suggest that writing *is* revision. While there are some forms of writing that rarely require revision (e.g. a shopping list) most writing requires some form of revision before being shared with other readers. In writing classrooms this can be done in groups (as members help each other to revise their work), but more commonly it will require writers to learn to revise their own work. This will be discussed in more detail later in the chapter.

Response to writing. An important element of any writing community is the function of response to the work of others. Members of any class need to learn how to respond critically to their peers while at the same time offering them encouragement and advice. The use of writing conferences is one effective way to ensure that this occurs. The writing conference is a structured opportunity for class members to read the work of peers and to respond in a variety of ways. The teacher has an important role to perform here as a model for response.

Publication and celebration of authorship. Writers also need the opportunity to publish their writing in a variety of forms for other readers. This is also often associated with a celebration of authorship when members of the writing community recognize the effort and achievement of others.

- *Writers need to be readers.*

As the above has probably suggested, good writers also read the work of others. Writers learn new styles for writing and acquire a variety of devices for making their writing clearer and more effective. All writers need to be active readers of literature and factual texts. The best writing classrooms are those where a good reading programme is also in place.

The writing workshop

The writing workshop is the name used by a number of educators (e.g. Calkins, 1986; Atwell, 1987) to describe the writing component of the English programme. The term is slightly misleading because in essence writing occurs across the curriculum. Almost all school subjects require writing. But the primary school teacher or secondary English teacher will still need to plan special writing times which provide much of the writing that will be discussed, and revised to develop the craft of writing.

In a primary school classroom most teachers who have a strong commitment to writing try to plan four to five sessions of 45 minutes' duration each week. Within this time students write, revise, conduct conferences, publish their work and engage in mini-lessons. I will describe conferences and mini-lessons later in this chapter, but I want to discuss the actual writing component of these lessons first. I have a number of basic requirements for writing in the writing workshop:

- First, writing is the primary activity in the writing workshop. Other things are still important, but they occupy less time and are there only to support writing.
- Second, all students keep their writing in a personal folder. Each piece of writing is dated, and all drafts of any piece are kept. All writing acts as a record of a writer's growth as well as a potential resource for future writing.
- Third, writers can choose their own topics.
- Fourth, all class members should do some writing in each workshop. Even when students are concentrating on publishing a piece of writing or having a conference with other writers, they are encouraged to find time for some writing.

In a typical writing workshop many things are going on at the same time. For example, a workshop might begin with a mini-lesson for everyone based on an aspect of someone's writing from the previous day. This might be followed by the class proceeding with a range of writing activities. For example, several students might be conducting a group conference, most might be drafting their latest piece, someone might be conducting research for a report, the teacher might be conducting roving conferences to check on student needs. The lesson might then finish with a whole class celebration of several students' recently published writing.

Providing support to writers

In Chapter 5 I used Wood, Bruner and Ross's six functions of scaffolding (in Rogoff, 1990) to describe my role as teacher in my grade 6 classroom that was centred on a literature-based approach to literacy. One of the keys to the changes I introduced as a teacher in my grade 6 classroom was my change in role in this classroom. My role was no longer based on the belief that student learning was simply the outcome of my teaching and the information I gave my students. Rather, the emphasis in my role came to be more predominantly the structuring of the learning environment so my students were able to participate more fully in decisions about their own learning and that of others. My key role was how to encourage my students to become more active managers of their own learning. Similarly, these same six functions can be applied to my role in writing. I will describe briefly how each function can be manifested:

- *Raising interest in writing.*
  This is achieved by:

  providing opportunities for students to share their writing with others;
  allowing students to exercise greater choice in their writing;
  regularly sharing quality writing with my students;
  reading to my class each day from a variety of text types, including literature and factual texts.

- *Simplifying the task of writing.*
  This is achieved by:

  helping my students to select topics and the most appropriate genre for writing;

providing help as part of the writing process in content, clarity and mechanics;

demonstrating the writing of a variety of written genres;

providing opportunities for joint construction of texts;

providing workshop mini-lessons on specific aspects of writing (described in detail later in the chapter).

- *Maintaining the pursuit of the goal.*
  This is achieved by:

  meeting with all students each week in individual conferences to talk about their writing;

  providing opportunities for group conferences;

  providing regular opportunities for publication and the celebration of authorship;

  encouraging students to keep a record of their writing;

  praising students who write regularly;

  making sure students are on task during writing sessions.

- *Noting inconsistencies in the children's writing.*
  This is achieved by:

  keeping detailed anecdotal records of student progress in writing;

  reminding students that they needed to write regularly;

  encouraging students to keep a personal record of their writing as well as new knowledge that has been acquired (e.g. knowledge of conventions);

  providing constructive criticism of their work through writing conferences (a function performed by the teacher and peers).

- *Controlling frustration and risk during problem solving.*
  This is achieved by:

  once again, creating a relaxed atmosphere that is not based on competition between students;

  encouraging students to attempt new topics, experiment with written genres, alternative media for writing, etc;

  offering constructive and supportive comments as students are involved in the writing process;

developing a class climate in which students (as well as the teacher) can contribute to the maintenance of this supportive environment.

- *Demonstrating the act of writing.*
  This is achieved by:

  reading to students every day in order to demonstrate the excitement of written language;

  demonstrating a variety of written genres using the overhead projector, sharing your own writing with the students, and writing in front of and with students.

The importance of the writing conference

Good writing will only emerge if students learn to revise their work (Cairney, 1981). Conferences are one vital way to help students develop the ability to revise and edit their work. They can take many different forms, varying in student composition and in purpose. The following are some of the options:

- Large group (or class) conferences
- Individual conferences
- Group conferences, teacher present
- Group conferences, teacher absent
- Revising with a partner
- Written comments from the teacher (conference from a 'distance').

CLASS LESSONS

Within every piece of writing produced in your classroom there exist numerous starting points for the introduction of revision strategies. You might:

- Read out a good line that someone has written.
- Share a well-chosen word.
- Place a piece of writing on the overhead projector to show how the writer has paragraphed, punctuated, started his story.
- Write a sentence on the board that someone has written and look at ways to improve it. (This must be done sensitively. A hint: use the work of your better writers, or ask for volunteers, stressing that 'We want to make your writing even better'.)

- Read a whole piece, commenting on the way it is structured, the way tension is developed, the way the writing 'hangs together' to form a complete piece of writing.

INDIVIDUAL PUPIL CONFERENCES

The individual conference is the starting point for the development of the ability to revise one's writing. It is at the individual level that teachers are best able to help children identify aspects of their own writing that would benefit from revision. The teacher's comments and questions will give the child a valuable insight into the revision process.

An essential rule in any such conference is that the teacher should, as much as possible, be positive. A teacher's comments might include:

- 'I like the use of the word muddle.'
- 'That's a good opening line.'
- 'That was beaut. You've taught me a lot about frogs.'
- 'I like the way you started that sentence.'
- 'You've paragraphed well. It's good to see that you start a new one for each new idea.'

Constructive criticism is also necessary. This might take the following forms:

- 'Read that to me again; I'm not sure what you meant. Could you tell me more?'
- 'The opening sentence is very important in any story. Your story might have been even better with a different lead-in sentence.'
- 'Read that the way it's written. Isn't something missing?'
- 'What word could have been used instead of "rain"?'
- 'It's hard for me to read and understand this first part; it's a very long sentence. Read it again and show me where you pause.'
- 'You've started these sentences the same way. How could you change some of them?'
- 'Do you need that sentence? Haven't you said that before?'

While these comments obviously relate to many elements in a piece of writing it would be undesirable to cover as many in a real conference. It is essential to concentrate on a limited number of features.

106

GROUP CONFERENCES

Initially, group conferences will involve a similar process to the individual conference, in that the teacher takes an active part. Groups will be formed in a variety of ways, using criteria such as friendship, interest, and ability. The teacher's role will involve directing the pupils' attention to specific aspects of the writing as well as eliciting responses through direct questioning.

A teacher's comments and questions might include:

- 'Notice how Adrian has started this sentence.'
- 'Isn't the sentence "the whales wallowed lazily in the water" a good one? Why?'
- 'What does Adrian's report tell us about whales?'
- 'How does this story make you feel?'
- 'How might Adrian have changed the final sentence in this story to make it even more interesting?'
- 'Has Adrian started a new paragraph each time he has started talking about a new idea?'
- 'Is that the way you spell "alligator"?'

Sometimes it is useful to group children according to need. It is then possible to examine specific aspects of a piece of writing. One piece of writing could initially be used for teacher-led discussion on aspects such as style, punctuation, usage, sentence structure.

Later groups might be asked to edit a piece of work alone with a specific purpose in mind. The purpose might be to:

- 'Read Allan's story then explain what it means to you. See if that's what he meant.'
- 'Check Bill's story to see if capital letters, full stops and commas are used when needed.'
- 'Read Sandra's story to see how well she has varied her sentence beginnings.' (It's just as useful to look at the positive.)
- 'Read Sue's story to check the spelling.'

Sometimes a group can be given a revision checklist. It is best if this is discussed and devised by the class with the teacher, rather than being imposed. Such a checklist might include:

- Does each sentence start with a capital and end with a full stop?
- Are the sentences clear?

- Have I left any words out or included unnecessary words?
- Have I used words correctly, e.g. was/were; is/are?
- Are there any words which should be checked for spelling?
- Is a new paragraph started for each new idea?
- Are the ideas in the correct sequence?
- Do the sentences start in a variety of ways?
- Are some words used too often?
- Does the story have a beginning, a middle, an end?
- Is it clear exactly what the writer means?
- Is more information needed to make the meaning clearer?
- Are the first and last sentences effective?
- Have words been used in unusual ways?

It is worth pointing out that while I have talked of revision as a process involving concern for both the surface features (proofreading) and the meaning conveyed, it is sometimes useful to ask children to separate the two aspects of the process in order to appreciate more clearly what is involved. This can be achieved by having separate proofreading and revision checklists.

INDIVIDUAL REVISION

As the child begins to accept greater responsibility for personal revision of writing, a class checklist such as the above can also be used individually. This will allow pupils to be continually reminded of special things to look for. Ideally, however, children should have their own individual checklist prepared jointly with their teacher.

In the early stages of individual revision process it is also useful to ask pupils to read their work to a partner or on to tape. This will still be a useful exercise even when the child is a proficient writer.

Children will also benefit from the keeping of a personal record of specific skills they have mastered. Some teachers would include also a list of skills they haven't mastered. However, as Graves (1984) points out, children already know what they *can't* do. Remind them of the things they *can* do.

The use of a personal dictionary will also serve as a useful aid to the young writer. Encourage your pupils to list words that they have problems with, perhaps even phrases, and then to mark them off when they become confident in their use.

Another important aid to the young writer are the written comments given by their teacher. A written comment, while not as effective as an individual conference, will still serve to give students valuable feedback concerning their writing. These comments should be as detailed and as positive as possible. Constructive criticism can also be given but usually only after something positive has been said. For example:

> A beaut short piece on the playground. A very good response to part of your school environment. It created images in my mind of life in a secondary school. An excellent sentence starting 'The world seemed to tremble'. I liked the fact that your piece was complete (writing, just like a painting, isn't much good if you leave parts of the work out). Well done Sharon. (written comments that the writer provided for a year 9 girl whose journal he read regularly)

Comments won't always be this detailed. Sometimes one word will do. Occasionally just a joke (this strengthens the relationship you have with your young writers) or a short comment might be placed near a specific part of the writing.

It is important to remember that revision of one's writing is difficult. Children will need a great deal of help from the teacher and from other writers (usually their peers). The above suggestions will provide useful assistance to many children as they attempt to master the skills in editing. It must be pointed out, however, that they won't always work for all children or teachers. Writers don't all revise in the same way. Some, for example, do most of their revising 'in their head'. For some, a second draft will involve scratching and scribbling, cutting and pasting, while for others it will mean a complete rewrite.

It is essential that a variety of strategies be used in any classroom to cater for the differences inherent in all young writers. Once again, we need to provide many pathways to writing.

Helping students to revise their writing

I believe that the major issue facing teachers in the 1990s is the need to help our students to revise their writing and hence to increase its 'quality'. As I outlined in Chapter 1, the 1980s saw unprecedented change in the teaching of writing in schools. Writing has been transformed in our schools, as the work of Graves, Murray, Britton, Emig and others has challenged teachers to examine and discard traditional practices. While it cannot be argued that there is now uniformity of approach in our classrooms (nor would one want this to occur), there have been a number of fundamental shifts in the way writing is taught. These changes can be summarized as follows:

We have seen the teaching of writing change…

FROM being…	*TO being…*
teacher centred	more child centred
topic based	more experience based
dominated by an emphasis on skills training in isolation	shaped by an emphasis on meaning, purpose and skills in context
product based	process (as well as product) based
directed by a teacher who was mainly a corrector	guided by a teacher whose many roles include that of a supporter, critic, listener, etc.
designed to get students to write for a single audience, i.e. teacher as examiner	designed to provide students with multiple 'real' audiences
predominantly restricted to writing for a single purpose, i.e. a one-shot 'composition' (usually a narrative)	designed to provide students with the opportunity to write for varied 'real' purposes

However, while there have been many changes in the way writing is taught, the challenge facing us now is how to make the next step Many teachers with whom I have worked will comment 'I have my children writing. They're keen, but how do I get them to revise their work and improve the quality of their piece?' Before answering such a question one needs to unpack what is meant by 'quality'.

Anyone who mentions the word 'quality' in an educational context deserves to be questioned. An obvious response is to ask: 'What do you mean by quality?' And rightly so, because when most people think of quality they are typically thinking just of the product. The numerous critics who have contributed articles and letters to every imaginable newspaper have typically shown a concern for spelling, punctuation and grammar. Furthermore, these writers (most of whom are without educational qualifications) have invariably suggested that children in the past produced writing of a higher quality than today's students.

While evidence does *not* exist to support the latter suggestion, it seems that many community members perceive that writing standards have fallen. However, one should not be surprised that this is the case, for all views of reality are social constructs. As Maturana (Maturana and Varella, 1987) has suggested, humans only come to know objective reality as members of a community.

Most critics seem to want to define quality in purely product-related terms. Quality for many is evidenced by specific observable characteristics within the surface features of one's writing. For a text to be classified as quality writing for these people, its spelling, word usage, sentence structure and text form must conform to their definition of conventionality.

Such a position is defensible of course, because all members of society are constantly being called upon to conform to socially constituted understandings, beliefs and values. What is indefensible is the arrogance of those who would suggest that their way is the only way, and their view of quality the only view of quality. Hence it is for social reasons that specific spellings are required, not because there is only one way to spell a word. And it is for social reasons that many see split infinitives (for example) as unacceptable. Bernard Shaw clearly understood this and made the following comments when confronted by someone who hated split infinitives:

> There is a busybody on your staff who devotes a lot of time to chasing split infinitives. Every good literary craftsman splits his infinitives when the sense demands it. I call for the immediate dismissal of this pedant. It is of no consequence whether he decides to go quickly, quickly to go, or to quickly go. The important thing is that he should go at once.

You might ask what has been the purpose of the above discussion? Are these simply the ramblings of another mad academic? Am I suggesting that spelling and grammatical 'correctness' are no longer necessary? No, not at all. What we need to do as teachers is recognize that we are educating children to take their place in society, and that there are socially constituted criteria (no matter how imprecise) to judge quality. Our students must take their place as individuals who need to function in specific social contexts, demanding conformity to certain standards. However, as I argued in Chapter 2, schooling needs also to be shaped by an awareness that students contribute to the shaping and development of language and culture.

As a teacher I believe I must help my students to produce quality writing. This inevitably means writing in a way that others find effective. However, being an effective writer requires more than conformity to socially defined conventions for the surface features of writing.

As teachers we need to examine the features of writing which are deemed by many to represent quality – that is, a standard of writing to which students should aspire. The question remains, is there such a set of features? In universal terms, I believe the answer is no. However, to respond to this truth by ignoring the fact that there are socially defined criteria for judging quality is rather irresponsible, and inevitably does our students a great disservice.

The critics of our children's writing are quick to share their limited criteria. What we must do as teachers is share, discuss and reflect upon our own (more complex) assumptions concerning quality. In the rest of this section of the chapter I want to share the criteria which I use for judging and encouraging quality writing. These criteria are those which I value, and which have shaped my interactions with children. I have never used them as a checklist, nor as a curriculum framework. However, I believe that my teaching of writing has at least intuitively been affected by these assumptions. In arriving at these broad generic criteria I have been influenced strongly by Murray (1982, 1984), although the ideas in no way should be attributed to him. I need to stress that this is just one way to define 'quality' and 'effectiveness'. For example, some educators would want to use linguistic criteria as a guide to teaching. Advocates of genre-based approaches (e.g. Christie, 1990) would be quick to suggest that what students need is the ability to effectively use specific genres. These educators would define quality as the ability to use these genres for a socially defined functional purpose. On the other hand I see genre as just one of the concerns of the teacher of writing. These issues will be discussed later in the chapter. The following represent the criteria which shape my interactions with students and their texts.

- *Does the writing achieve its purpose?*
This first criterion is of paramount importance, for if a piece of writing does not achieve its original purpose it matters little whether it

has been spelled or punctuated correctly. One of the weaknesses of process critics who would want to return to the 'good old days' is that in the good old days little thought was given to writing purpose in the classroom. There was only one purpose – write this well for the teacher. 'Process writing' has made teachers and students far more aware of the many purposes that writing can have.

As children do begin to write for a variety of real purposes (e.g. to reflect on personal experience by using a diary, to record observations, to write a science report which has the potential to teach someone else something) one can attempt to apply this most basic criterion. For some writing it is the only criterion of use. For example, how does one evaluate a diary? Only the writer can do this, and the only point worthy of assessment is whether it has achieved its purpose. How else would one evaluate the impromptu funeral order of service for two dead mice shown in Figure 6.1? This piece was written by a small group of children aged 3 to 7 years who had found several dead mice in the back yard of their house. They decided that a funeral had to be planned. The text that resulted was written without adult help and was essentially an order of service.

- *Does it have originality and freshness?*
This is a more difficult criterion to define. How does one make such a judgement? Since reading is a constructive process (Cairney, 1990b) originality and freshness must be very much in the 'eye (mind) of the beholder'. But as a reader, there is one thing that I loathe – reading things which elicit a reading little different from previous readings. It matters little whether it is a university text on research methods; or a piece of poetry – one wants to encounter at least a spark of originality and freshness whenever one reads.

Children have some strange notions concerning originality. Many equate it purely with content and tend to think original content is always something that is out of one's everyday world. This may well be a learned behaviour, the result of well-meaning creative writing teachers. Hence, a story about a trip to Mars is frequently seen as original, fresh and creative, but a poem about a cup of coffee is not. However, Peter Grosse (a grade 3 student) thought otherwise when he wrote the poem on p. 115 (Figure 6.2).

This is not to suggest that originality means writing about new things all the time. Originality should not be restricted to content,

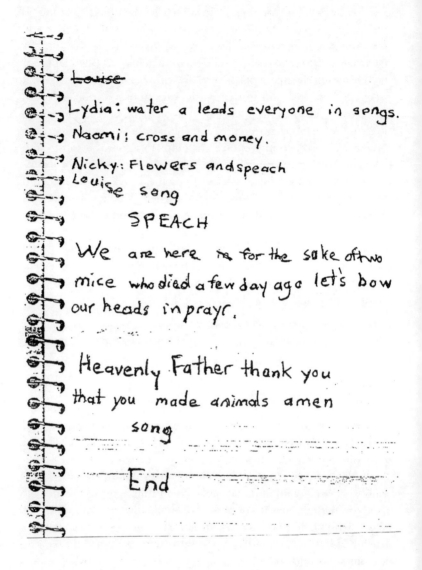

Lydia: water a leads everyone in songs.
Naomi: cross and money.
Nicky: Flowers and speach
Louise song
        SPEACH
We are here for the sake of two
mice who died a few day ago let's bow
our heads in prayr.

Heavenly Father thank you
that you made animals amen
        song
        End

Figure 6.1 An order of service for the funeral of two mice

although it does concern content. It also relates to the writer's style, word choice, text form, use of literary and illustrative devices and so on. Of course, having said this, one now needs to make the comment that what is fresh and original for one may not be for another. Notions of freshness and originality cannot be separated from the complex interplay between reader and text.

Coffee

Peter Grosse,
Year 3,
Lutheran School.

I love you coffee,
You make me glow.
You make me smile,
I love you so,
My nerves don't like you,
But what do they know?
I love you coffee,
I love you so.

Figure 6.2 A poem written by a grade 3 boy, entitled 'Coffee'

- *Is it focused writing?*

Focus is another criterion that is difficult to define, because once again the success of the writer depends partly upon the success of the reader. Focused writing has a central concern, and maintains this throughout. It is this central concern which gives the text unity and helps to fulfil its purpose. For example, a piece of argumentative writing about the justifiability of whaling needs to maintain its focus if readers are to be engaged. Similarly, a letter of application for a job cannot afford to meander off on to matters peripheral to the essential criteria for the position.

I can vividly recall reading an application for the position of Child Care Centre Director and shaking my head in disbelief when I came to a paragraph in which the applicant wrote that 'my friends say I am an attractive and bouncy lady', and 'I like scuba diving and have lots of personality'. The writer had lost sight of the focus of the application and its purpose.

- *Does the writer show authority over topic?*

Good writing also requires the writer to know his/her topic. Whether it's a report on a science experiment, a piece of historical fiction, or a poem about daffodils, the writer needs to know about the topic. But authority has another dimension. A writer also needs to show the reader that he/she has something vital to say – that the writer is in control. Bruce Catton said that the quality he looked for in any kind of writing is

> that of complete sincerity and earnestness. The writer must have something he wants to communicate. (in Bates, 1989, p. 5)

- *Is it well-structured?*

All writing requires logical structure. Just as consistently structured sentences help readers to read, so too a well-structured text helps the reader to construct meaning. Considerate texts have logical and predictable structure.

We come to expect texts of a particular type to have a consistent structure. We know how most fairy stories begin, and how the plot develops, because we have encountered their text structures before. In the same way, when we read a report we expect it to be structured in a specific way. This is not to say that writers cannot vary structures, nor make up their own (some authors do so deliberately for effect), but generally, consistency is desirable.

- *Has language been used well?*

Good writing, irrespective of form, requires the writer to use the best possible words in the best possible order. Sometimes a special word is required, but frequently a simple word is more powerful. Somerset Maugham said that:

> To write simply is as difficult as to be good. (in Bates, 1989, p. 5)

Similarly, Colin Thiele has stressed in numerous public addresses and interviews that his aim when writing is to use simple words wherever possible. When simple words are used well, writing has a special power. When compiling an anthology of children's poetry and prose

(Cairney, 1988b), I encountered a piece of writing contributed by a fifth grade boy that used words to such effect that the reading of it turned my stomach. This child's piece shows how language can be used with great power.

An excerpt from

BATTLEFIELD

Thomas Whitaker
Year 5
Eurongilly Primary

As the sun comes up as if on cue the heavy artillery stops its booming only to be replaced by the crackling of machine gun fire. The light brings the awful sight of dead and dying men, mud, blood and forests of 'barbed wire'. The musty smell of gunpowder is everywhere. Every now and then the scene blazes with the flames of a flamethrower. The screams of dying men and "stretcher stretcher" are everywhere.

All of a sudden the booming of heavy artillery fills the air. It goes on for a few minutes before stopping as suddenly as it started. A brave young boy of about eight is now, out of spite being slowly bayonetted. Starting from his feet they are now up to his thighs. I know what must be done. I raise my rifle, feeling sick in the stomach as the boy's screams reach my ears, I pull the trigger. The boy's screams for mercy stop, cut off.

The enemy are cursing because their fun has been ruined. An ugly smile twists on the leader's face as he spots me. I raise my rifle bringing the man's head into the rifle's scope. I recock the gun and fire. Recock. Fire. Recock. Fire. A pattern that has killed millions of people. The man falls down, dead. His comrades cry out in fury. They start running towards me. I recock, fire, recock, fire. That murdering pattern again. Recock. Fire. Three more of the enemy lie dead before me.

Figure 6.3 A piece of writing by a grade 5 student, entitled 'Battlefield'

- *Is it tight writing?*

Another essential requirement for writing is that words should be used economically. This may seem related to the last point but is slightly different. It concerns the efficient use of language. Writers tighten their texts after they have worked out what they have to say. It is at this stage that the writer attempts to remove repetitive sentence beginnings, redundancies and overused words. Macrorie (1985) calls one form of the latter 'whooery, whichery and thatery'.

For me as a reader, the following would be seen as a sloppy sentence: 'Jason was a brave boy and he was a strong boy and he was also never afraid.' This sentence could be tightened to read: 'Jason never showed fear; he was brave, tough and strong.' Katrina Webb's piece 'Termite revenge' is a piece of tight writing (Figure 6.4).

Supporting writers through mini-lessons

It is one thing to recognize quality in writing, but another thing to develop it in young writers. The teacher has a vital role to play in the development of writer's revision strategies. But how is this to be done? While writers learn many things through the experience of writing, teachers need to provide scaffolding support if they are to learn how effectively to use revision strategies, and if they are to become confident using a variety of written genres.

I have already discussed the role that conferences play earlier in this chapter. What I want to do now is provide an insight into how focused attention can be given to specific aspects of the craft of writing.

To do this, the concept of mini-lessons (Calkins, 1986) is helpful. For Calkins, a mini-lesson involves a brief meeting that begins a writing workshop (or lesson) in which the whole class addresses an issue that has arisen in a previous workshop or in a student's piece of writing. These mini-lessons could focus on a simple copy-editing issue like punctuation, or they could focus on the introduction of a new genre or a sophisticated revision strategy. The purpose of the mini-lesson is for the teacher (or other students) to share personal knowledge of writing.

Atwell (1987) suggests that the mini-lesson creates a communal frame of reference. For her, many of the mini-lessons are procedural and are used to demonstrate to students how to interact with each other, find topics, etc. For me the mini-lesson is more focused on the revision of writing and is conducted both as a class and also in small groups. The concept of the mini-lesson used in this book has the following dimensions:

TERMITE REVENGE

Katrina Webb, Year 5,
St Patricks Primary School. (Holbrook).

Sam crossed the paddock angrily. He had been in a bad temper at school and had got into trouble for answering (more like shouting) back at the teacher.

As he crossed a mound of dirt in the sown field he noticed that a swarm of small red termites were crossing back and forth carrying food from the paddock to their home. Winter was coming and they were stacking their food away to be ready.

Sam thought back to his father's calm words "If you're not going to help, then at least get rid of that nasty temper". He'd shouted back at his father "I'll do whatever I like, and no-one, not even hell, can stop me. I swear you'll never find me." He had then stormed out of the house.

Now here he was alone in the paddock. A wind lifted Sam's long fringe of hair, revealing dark angry brows. A harsh winter wind cut sharply through his clothes. Suddenly Sam felt afraid. He looked around at the trees, but home was a long way away, and he would seem cowardly if he went back, being only out for a couple of hours.

Out of anger he kicked the home of the termites and stormed over it, breaking it to bits and squashing thousands of termites with his heavy gumboots. Then finally satisfied, Sam turned to look at the remaining mound and bugs. He smiled wickedly and sat down on a log to watch what they'd do.

Suddenly a line of something red came pouring out of the battered termite home.

Sam stood up in horror, as the giant sized termites came rushing towards him. He gasped in an unearthly-like pitch, and collapsed onto the ground. With a last feeble breath he remembered his sworn oath "I swear no-one will ever find me." The termites swarmed over his mouth and eyes, sticking tight and filling his throat. "No, no, no" Sam gasped.

"That stupid boy, I'll never find him." muttered his dad stomping over an old deserted termite mound.

Figure 6.4 Katrina's text entitled 'Termite revenge'

- The cycle of activities within the mini-lesson does not follow a prescribed sequence.
- The mini-lessons are planned at the point of need and reflect student strengths as well as weaknesses in writing.
- While the teacher is often at the centre of interactions in mini-lessons, all students are encouraged to engage and at times students will lead the discussion.
- The mini-lesson can be conducted with the whole class, a group, or even an individual.
- The content of mini-lessons varies depending on student need.
- The duration of mini-lessons can vary from several minutes to almost half an hour.

In the rest of this section I want to share a number of mini-lessons that were used in my classrooms.

MINI-LESSON 1 – ADDING FACTS TO ONE'S WRITING

During a writing workshop that I was running in a 'borrowed' grade 5 class Louise was writing a piece about life in England in the nineteenth century. She read her first draft to me and asked for comments. My response went something like this:

> I like this piece, Louise. It's a great topic. I've always liked historical fiction (Have you read *Playing Beatie Bow*?) and you've obviously tried to make this accurate historically. It's a great first line, but you could do with some more details (some extra facts). For example, exactly where is this set? What type of street is it? What is the house like? Are they rich people or poor people? Maybe you need to add some more facts to make it come alive.

Louise went away and redrafted her piece (Figure 6.5 shows the first and second draft of part of this piece). Her second draft had been elaborated, additional facts provided, and more of the context revealed.

Later I reused this example with the whole class because the problems observed in Louise's piece were common to most writers. The mini-lesson planned owes much to Macrorie's (1985) writing techniques. I started the lesson by reading some of Leon Garfield's story *Fair's Fair* (1981). We talked about this text, and I stressed that it is filled with facts that help it to come alive.

To make my point more forcefully I wrote a simple sentence on the board – SHARON SAT IN THE CHAIR – and dramatized five different ways that this sentence could be interpreted. We discussed each of these interpretations and I stressed that readers need some facts if they are to interpret the context in a way that the author intended. We also discussed the problem of texts overloaded with facts and the need to write sometimes in a way that allows multiple interpretations. I then provided the class with another sentence – JACK OPENED THE PARCEL – and invited specific students to provide dramatic interpretations.

After this, I showed the group the first draft of the piece Louise had written and explained that she had been trying to improve it by adding more facts. I asked the students to close their eyes and imagine the scene. After approximately two minutes I asked them to

The year was 1853 in London England.
The streets were crowded with carts.
Above the crowd was a boy looking out
the window of his fathers house.

The year was 1853 in London England
The streets were crowded with carts
carring carring vegtables, hay and
other goods to sell. They clopped
along the cobble stone streets.
Pauppers dressed in dirty ragged
clothes ran across the road
chasing a mouse. Above the bustling
crowd was a boy looking out of the
window of his fathers house a beauty-
ful mansion, with a knee rug over
his legs. It was Henry Severin. In
the warmth of the fire he sat watching
the peasants freeze in the cold snow

Figure 6.5 Louise's redrafted writing

share some of the details of their images. What was the street like? The house? Were they rich or poor? How old was the boy? Why was he there?

As a group we then attempted to write a different version. Following this joint construction we looked at Louise's piece. We examined the way we (and Louise) had changed the text and reflected upon the impact that the new facts had for us as readers.

Finally, I asked my students to choose a piece of their draft writing and suggested that they reread it, underlining sections where facts could be added. When the texts had been read and the generalizations (needing revision) identified, the drafts were discussed with a partner. Students then attempted to rewrite selected sections and shared them once again, seeking a reader's opinion about the effectiveness of the changes.

MINI-LESSON 2 – USING METAPHOR

This mini-lesson had its beginnings following a minor comment I made about part of a text that was being read for enjoyment to a year 6 class. During the reading of *A Handful of Thieves* by Nina Bawden (1967) I commented upon the sentence

> 'London was a greedy sponge', Dad said once, 'sopping up towns like water.'

I explained that this was a metaphor and read on. Some days later a student included a wonderful simile in a narrative, 'the farmer's face was like a dried up prune'. I asked the student to share this with the rest of class then contrasted it with the metaphor from Bawden's story that had been encountered several days before. I then introduced the class to rhyming couplets (e.g. 'TV on such a noise/ Screaming squawking grotty boys') and suggested that they might write some.

Several days later a student included a wonderful metaphor in a narrative: 'The principal was a rabbit trap lying in wait for his next innocent victim.' Again, it was shared and links made with previous lessons.

In literature sharing sessions that took place in subsequent lessons other links were made to our discussions on metaphor and examples of similes and metaphors discussed.

On another occasion, while teaching a group of grade 5 and 6 children I stopped to talk to Roslyn as she drafted a new piece about a fairly obnoxious friend. I read the piece and responded to the draft in general terms, then asked Roslyn to read the lead out loud. It seemed to me as a reader to be a pretty dull start to a lively Judy Blume-type narrative. I asked her whether she felt the lead did justice to the action of the story that was to follow. I asked Roslyn to think about other ways she could start the piece and to experiment with alternatives. When I returned five minutes later she had drafted three possibilities (Figure 6.6).

Roslyn's Leads

Original Opening

It all started that misty morning as I was hurrying down the hall to my locker when I bumped into Amelia Rynehart the snob of the school.

1. **I started it all when I bumped into Amelia Rynehart while hurrying down the hall to my locker.**

2. **"I hate you," I called as Amelia Rynehart the snob of the school bumped into me knocking me over.**

3. **"Some people think they're great. Parading down the hall knocking people over," I moaned to my friend as she helped pick my bruised body off the ground.**

Figure 6.6 Roslyn's redrafted leads

I discussed the leads with Roslyn and asked her which one she preferred. She chose the third and proceeded to rewrite the piece. In a later lesson this once again became the basis for a group lesson for students who also needed help with lead writing.

The above examples provide some indication of the way in which mini-lessons are used to improve students' ability to revise their writing. It is important to note that a mini-lesson is not a prescriptive sequence of steps, nor is it a recipe for developing quality writing.

Essentially it is a pattern of interaction within my classroom, a framework for talking about text.

The mini-lessons outlined are typical of many that I have introduced with students who I have taught. The content of these lessons varies, as do the participants and methods. Also, the cycle is never the same. For example, we do not always jointly construct text. Furthermore, there is no clear starting point for the cycle of activities. Two of the above examples commence with talk about texts that students have written. The third example, on the other hand, begins with the reading of a piece of literature (demonstration) and moves quickly to talk about this literary text.

The degree of teacher involvement in the cycle also varies greatly. In the above examples the teacher has a major role. At other times the teacher is far less on centre stage. This variation is in keeping with the purpose of the writing, the students concerned and the degree of pupil support available.

Genre theory and writing – does it have anything to offer?

A genre is a specific type of writing. Within the field of literature the term has been used primarily of literary genres, for example, poetry, novel, short story, drama; or perhaps, more specifically, legend, fable, fairy tale, historical fiction, science fiction, epic poetry, the ode and so on (Cairney, 1992b).

But the use that is applied more recently to the word 'genre' by linguists is far more specific. The term is used to refer to a 'social process which has some purpose' (Collerson, 1988, p. 12). Genres arise within a specific social context. A court hearing, church service or family meal could be considered genres. These genres may have variations from one event to another, but over multiple uses of specific genres (e.g. a church service) there are certain predictable elements, and an accepted sequence of activities (Collerson, 1988). The reason for this is that the activities are carried out with a specific purpose or goal in mind.

Christie (1985) describes genres in this way:

> ... any staged and culturally purposive activity leading to the creation of a text ... to serve different social purposes. (p. 12)

Recent interest in genre theory reflects the belief by a number of linguists and educators that teachers who might classify themselves as 'whole language' teachers inadvertently neglect giving attention to specific knowledge about language, which, linguists argue, is empowering.

The following (with acknowledgement, in part, to Sawyer and Watson, 1987) is a summary of their major concerns:

- Genres ought to be consciously chosen by writers and their writing made to conform to the particular genre's structure.
- Structures of genres ought to be taught to pupils so that they will model their writing on the genre structure.
- There is too much emphasis on narrative form in primary schools and this is a poor preparation for working in the expository modes required by secondary schools and more importantly the outside world.
- Teachers have a responsibility to make the features of language explicit to their students.

Since this debate first surfaced in the mid-1980s, there have been many books written about genre-based approaches, curricula have been modified to accommodate genre theory, and teaching packages have been designed and sold. Thankfully, there is now far more common ground concerning the importance of knowledge about language than there was five years ago. Nevertheless, a number of issues still remain unresolved, and I continue to have a number of concerns with this approach to teaching writing. Let me describe each of these in turn.

My first concern relates to the danger of genres being seen as unchanging. Identifying genres seems simple enough. But if one attempts to define a genre, it is assumed that one will need to define its elements. I question how uniform genres are over time, from situation to situation, from one use to another (even by the same writer). To define them too dogmatically is to run the risk of imposing on writers sanitized forms. The history of writing suggests that genres change, and at times are deliberately modified for writer effect.

A second concern is that once one identifies genres it is logical that some would want to teach them. But how (more on this later)? And when does this instruction occur? I have grave concerns that attempts to teach genres will lead to decontextualized lessons about language with control being wrested away from our students.

Third, I also have concerns about any approach that has the potential to place form and structure before meaning. The field of education is riddled with legacies to instructional approaches which foregrounded specific aspects of language, for example the teaching of grammar, spelling instruction and story grammar, to name just a few.

Fourth, I have doubts concerning the assumption that there has been too much emphasis on narrative form. The work of Britton *et al.* (1975), Martin *et al.* (1976) and Barnes (1976) has suggested that learning is facilitated when students are allowed to use their own language rather than being forced to conform to the particular language conventions of specific subject areas. Added to this is the work of Graves (1984), which has shown that children write with greater power when given 'control' of their writing.

Fifth, I also question the assumption of genre theorists that genres can only be acquired if they are taught explicitly. Language work by people like Gordon Wells (1986) has shown how the functions of language develop at a very early age. Others, like Jerry Harste (see Harste *et al.*, 1984), have shown that written genres begin to appear during the very beginnings of literacy.

It is my view that we are still somewhat diverted from the real issues concerning genre-based approaches. I want to suggest that there are two major issues: how explicit should we be when talking about language?; how should we interact with our students as they write?

In the early work of linguists like Martin *et al.* (1987) there seemed to be a lack of concern with pedagogy. The approaches that were being suggested were very teacher-centred and text-based. Since that time the work of educators like Derewianka (1990) has redressed this deficiency to some extent. Whole language advocates argued about the manner in which genre became a focus for classroom discussion. Some of the major criticisms of genre-based approaches included the danger that a focus on genre might lead to control being taken away from the child concerning learning, with classrooms becoming more teacher-centred rather than child-centred. This in turn, it has been argued, can lead to a focus on the reproduction of other people's language rather than the construction of one's own.

One of the most interesting arguments has surrounded the issue of how children learn about language. Whole language advocates have been accused of assuming that knowledge of language is acquired by a process of 'osmosis'. However, no one who has ever been in a whole language classroom could seriously suggest this.

However, while readers and writers do not learn about written language simply by 'osmosis', they do learn a great deal about language simply from the experience of reading and writing. The work of Harste *et al.* (1984) has shown clearly that even the very young child learns a great deal about language through immersion. Nevertheless, we learn even more as we interact with others concerning our reading and writing. As I have already outlined above, we need to provide opportunities for our students to discuss writing in a variety of contexts (e.g. mini-lessons, individual conferences, group conferences, class groups, partners, etc.).

In recent years I have spent a lot of time reflecting upon the way whole language teachers talk to students about text. The critical element of this talk is that there is always a central concern with meaning. That is, while the teacher might be directing student attention to some feature of written language (including genre), this is always within the context of a concern to construct meaning as one writes or reads. Furthermore, the focus on language is rarely an end in itself. It almost always serves the purpose of making meaning.

The teacher's role as part of this text talk is a complex scaffolding process involving close interaction, not simply instruction from a detached expert. As he/she interacts with students a number of specific functions are performed, typically, in a cyclical way. These functions include:

- *Offering information* if the student has gaps in knowledge that are of vital importance to a purposeful task with which he/she is engaged.
- Being an *Interested listener*.
- Acting as a *Strategy suggester* if the student's existing strategies are not working.
- *Sharing* of insights, successes, and problems experienced from reading and writing.
- *Supporting* the student's efforts by offering constructive feedback.
- Serving as a *Critical fellow language learner* when student perform-

ance is not up to expectations, when effort has not been applied, or when the point has been missed.

- *Introducing* new language forms, new authors, new uses for writing, alternative writing styles, new language, writing topics, different purposes for writing, new audiences and so on.
- *Demonstrating* real and purposeful reading and writing.

It is clear that the concept of genre as outlined by linguistics is of use for classroom teachers. While linguists will say that classroom teachers need to come to grips with functional grammar as a foundation for all teaching, I am yet to be convinced that this is necessary, or even desirable. However, it must be stressed that text genre is one aspect of language that needs consideration. It is not the central component of language, nor should it be the central part of any literacy programme.

For students to achieve the writing purposes they see as legitimate, they need to understand what written genres are and in which social contexts they should be used. The teacher's task is to support writers as they learn more about the genres of language.

As explained above, our role as teachers of writing is a complex one; we need to be many things to many students.

Getting started

Just as it took a catalyst to transform my grade 6 reading classroom (on that occasion a Core Library, and a copy of Don Holdaway's *Independence in Reading*), so too, if one wants to make major changes to one's writing programme, there is a need for a starting point. But before I outline how to get started, it is important to stress once again that what I have been discussing above has been far more than a new methodology for writing. Rather, I have been outlining a model for the development of a community of learners.

So, where do we start? What could be the beginning point for a change from a classroom environment in which the way I have taught writing has been more consistent with a teacher-centred skills-based approach to teaching?

The short answer is that first one needs to rethink one's assumptions about writing and one's role in its development. Once again, a variety of starting points could be adopted. The following is one suggestion.

On a designated day (which you have announced at least a week in advance) introduce your students to the concept of the writing workshop. In doing this it is important to talk about how you taught writing previously and state why you are changing. On this day you might:

- Hand out writing folders (plain A4 manilla folders) on which is written each student's name. Inside, students might place a heading on the left-hand inside cover which says 'Ideas for writing topics'. On the right-hand side might be written 'Writing I have completed'.
- Explain how each writing workshop will work and suggest that the first three days will be mainly used for an introduction to the writing workshop.
- Ask students to discuss with a neighbour what they might write about. To begin this discussion you might suggest that they can write about anything, and that it could be real or imaginary and in any form. Typically, I follow this by demonstrating on an overhead projector how I brainstorm possible topics. All the time I do this I explain out loud my reasons for making the choices I do.
- At the beginning of the second writing workshop, start by explaining that writing conferences will be a normal part of each workshop for some people. Show them a roster for group conferences and begin to meet with groups to discuss the topic brainstorming from the previous workshop. Have other students take a topic and begin draft writing.
- At the beginning of the third workshop conduct a whole class mini-lesson, either using topics generated from previous workshops, or using a piece of draft writing to examine a fairly basic aspect of writing (e.g. writing good lead sentences).
- By the second week you should mention to your students that one of the aims in the writing workshop will be to publish pieces of writing at regular intervals in a variety of forms for other readers. It is useful at this point to show them published writing from another class and to read some sample pieces.
- At the commencement of one of the workshops in the second week it is also useful to explain what writers are to do with draft material. This mini-lesson is largely procedural and should focus

129

on dating drafts, storing them properly and maintaining the writing folder.

- By the third week most students should be working on a piece of writing and should basically understand how the writing workshop is conducted. All students should now have had at least one group conference and all students should now be meeting regularly for individual conferences. It is at this point that you should begin to keep detailed anecdotal records of student progress, conferences and mini-lessons. This will form the basis of student assessment in writing. This will be discussed in greater detail in Chapter 7.

- In the fourth or fifth week you might also introduce students to the idea of an individual revision checklist. Explain to them that this is to be kept inside their writing folder and is designed to help them with self-revision. Suggest that they try to identify two features of their writing that regularly appear to be the focus of revision. Discuss those features selected in group conferences during this week and help students to confirm the features of their writing to which they give special attention in future weeks. Once the checklist is established it is regularly evaluated and revised. Features are deleted as students cease to have problems with them and others are added as the need arises.

- Some teachers also introduce a range of other embellishments to the writing workshop. For example, you might later introduce a personal dictionary for each student, in which he or she places words which frequently cause problems. Other teachers provide each student with a journal in which to record ideas for writing, special interests, reflections on experiences and books that have been read, interesting language use, newspaper clippings, etc. In younger grades some teachers set up writing ideas boxes (collections of topics, pictures, objects to write about), word banks for student use, etc.

Once the ground rules are outlined and the writing workshop is in operation you will need to constantly monitor student progress and the effectiveness of all aspects of the programme. It is important that adjustments are made and procedural problems clarified as they occur. In this way the writing workshop will be more successful.

Conclusion

The advent of 'process writing' was responsible for a dramatic increase in the importance of writing, and brought significant changes in the way it was taught. The above discussion of writing has been designed to challenge teachers to rethink the way they teach writing. Our role as teachers of writing is a complex one; we need to be many things to many students. As I have indicated above, we are sharers, strategy suggesters, information givers, questioners, reactors, listeners and so on. All of these major tasks are related in one significant way; each is designed to help create a community of writers – that is, a group of people who read and write for real purposes and who talk freely about their reading and writing because it is an important part of their world (as described in Chapter 2).

In Chapter 7 I want to look more closely at another important element in the creation of effective literacy learning environments – assessment and evaluation. I want to explore how assessment is integral to the teaching and learning of writing and reading and the creation of exciting literacy environments.

Assessing literacy learning

In this chapter I want to talk about assessment and evaluation. For some literacy educators assessment and evaluation are a passion. I have to admit that I cannot understand this preoccupation because as a teacher I have always viewed assessment as an integral part of the teaching/learning process. While the data we collect certainly 'drive' the teaching/learning process, these are simply part of teaching and learning, and should never become the focus of our attention. Assessment serves teaching; it should never be the other way around. If the latter does occur then one must question the assumptions that are directing the teaching/learning process.

The first issue to address in this chapter is that of definitions. Those who see assessment as 'everything' tend to delight in inventing new terms to add confusion to the teacher's world. While I will not even attempt to describe all of the terms available, I want to define the terms I will use in this chapter. I will begin by examining what I mean by the terms assessment, evaluation, monitoring, observations, indicators, profiles, and reporting.

Definition of terms

Assessment is the act or process of gathering data concerning the products and processes of literacy in order to make judgements of student learning, especially in relation to needs, strengths, abilities and achievements.

Evaluation is judgement of performance based on monitoring and assessment information that has been gathered. It has two main forms, summative, which is a determination of the degree to which the objectives of learning have been met, and formative, which is the monitoring of student progress. Evaluation is a process that has relevance also for judgements about the effectiveness of teaching programmes.

Monitoring is the observation made during the process of implementation of a planned topic, lesson or task. It is a description of the literacy behaviour of one's students and usually leads to adjustment within the teaching learning programme. It usually involves the teacher
in a non-participatory way and draws on a number of successive
learning situations and pieces of work. It also includes unexpected
observations, and is usually recorded in the form of a profile.

Observation is the detailed and focused attention to the ways in which
individuals or groups of students participate in learning tasks. Information is usually recorded in the form of anecdotal records,
checklists, or portfolios.

Indicators are pieces of information about the performance of a student.
They can be expressed as benchmarks or expected outcomes and are
usually goal oriented. They can be monitored at regular intervals
and compared to one or more standards. They are an integral part
of evaluation.

Profiles are a collection of indicators of student performance. They
draw together several aspects of growth and development in order to
guide educators in ongoing assessment.

Reporting is a term that usually refers to the more formal process of
providing information for others with an interest in a child's learning. While this is often the parent, students also have a vital interest
in process, as do future teachers, who may use this information (if
available) as the starting point for their own assessment and evaluation of individuals.

In this chapter my focus will be primarily on assessment, for this is
the key to good evaluation and reporting. Reference will also be made
to monitoring, observation, profiles and indicators to show how each
is related to the more central processes of assessment and evaluation.

As well as the above well-known terms, there have been a number
of new terms introduced as educators have tried to find more appropriate ways to describe our changed assessment and evaluation practices. For example, Cambourne and Turbill (1990) and Hancock
et al. (1994) talk about *responsive evaluation*, which they acknowledge
grew out of the work of Stake (1975) and Guba and Lincoln (1981).
This term is used to highlight the belief that evaluation should be

oriented to programme activities rather than intents, should respond to audience requirements for information, and should recognize different values and perspectives. Valencia *et al.* (1994) have introduced the term *authentic assessment* to stress the need for any assessment practice to capture 'authentic uses' of literacy in and outside the classroom. Finally, Woodward (1993) uses the term *negotiated evaluation* to convey the sense that evaluation should involve interaction between participants (children, teachers and parents), be based on data collected from multiple sources, and keep all participants well informed. While all of these terms have merit, I do not intend to use them; rather, I will stick to the traditionally used terms as already defined.

Some principles for assessment

I will talk most about assessment in this chapter because I see it as the central and overarching practice that informs teaching and allows evaluations to be made. As the above definition indicates, assessment is the act or process of gathering data concerning the products and processes of literacy in order to make judgements of student learning, especially in relation to needs, strengths, abilities and achievements.

Teachers should be constantly engaged in a process of data collection. Teachers are essentially researchers constantly seeking data to support or refute the thousands of hypotheses (hunches if you will) that give direction to their teaching day by day. But it is clear that what I mean by assessment may be different from what another teacher means by assessment. Would I be happy with any kind of data? No! And would I be happy to see data collected in any way? No! So, let me first outline the basic principles that guide my assessment and evaluation processes. Obviously these principles are reflective of all that I have said in the previous chapters of this book concerning literacy and learning. While the comments that follow are mine, the principles are reflective of the work of Valencia *et al.* (1990). While I cannot attribute the ideas to these authors, my thinking has been clarified by reading their work.

- *Assessment should be based on the observation of 'whole' language in action.*
It is important to recognize at the outset that assessments of literacy should recognize the 'wholeness' of language in all its form. That is, literacy is part of language and as such does not stand alone. For

example, every act of writing is at once also an act of reading and in most cases leads to talking and listening as work is shared. Furthermore, when one attempts to assess any aspect of literacy, it is important always to recognize that if we isolate one part of the product or process from its full context then we are no longer observing an authentic act of literacy.

- *Assessment is integral to teaching and learning.*
The first thing to stress about assessment is that it is not something external to teaching and learning; rather, it is an integral part. Some people conceive assessment as something someone does to someone else from 'outside' the situation. Assessment involves observation and data collection by participants (the teacher, students and parents) as part of the learning process.

- *Assessment should be continuous.*
Assessment needs also to be continuous. We should be continually seeking data on student learning. While we may at times plan observations as part of the assessment process at specific intervals in a unit of learning or during a typical day, we nevertheless need to view assessment as continuous and cumulative. That is, we build up an increasingly more complete picture of the student as learner.

- *Assessment should be multidimensional.*
It is also important for assessment to be multidimensional. That is, it should be based on data derived from a variety of sources and dealing with varying dimensions of literacy. The classroom teacher will observe reading and writing products and processes in varied forms which are used for varying purposes. Effective assessment will also involve seeking the students' and the parents' perspectives on learning.

- *Assessment should be collaborative.*
As the above point has implied, assessment should be a collaborative process, involving students, teachers and parents. This will include collaborating to negotiate the form that assessment will take, the evidence that learning has occurred (or not) and the use to which data are put.

- *Assessment should be grounded in knowledge.*
All assessment is dependent on a solid base of knowledge of literacy. The early chapters of this book were written to provide a clear know-

ledge base for what was to follow. Effective assessment flows from a good understanding of the nature of the reading and writing processes, as well as how students learn.

- *Assessment should be authentic.*

As Valencia *et al.* (1994) have argued, all assessment should be 'authentic'. That is, it should be based on assessment activities that represent the literacy behaviour of the community and workplace and that are reflective of teaching and learning in and outside the classroom. Far too often assessment has been based on tests and activities that are not reflective of the literacy practices of the classroom and/or the outside world.

- *Assessment should inform students and lead to new directions in teaching.*

Finally, it seems almost unnecessary to suggest that assessment should inform students, parents and teachers and lead to more effective learning outcomes for all, but it needs to be said. Good assessment should result in better teaching, and students who are aware of their own strengths, abilities and needs in literacy.

A framework for assessment in literacy

Armed with the above principles I want to suggest a framework for literacy assessment in the classroom. For some, assessment is a one-dimensional linear process as depicted opposite (Figure 7.1). A teacher begins with a set of expectations that are influenced by syllabuses, national curricula, prior teaching experiences and school and community expectations. Using this information, the teacher plans a sequence of learning tasks then evaluates them. This then feeds back into one's expectations and the cycle continues.

While some teachers actually programme in this linear way, I want to suggest that such an impoverished view of assessment is very limiting. As my comments above have already indicated, I see assessment as a far more intricate process which is integral to teaching and learning. The process I envisage is not linear, but rather is recursive in nature. A number of writers have talked of assessment as a 'cycle' in order to understand the recursiveness of this process. This concept owes much to the work of Graves (1983) and Harste *et al.* (1985). In a more recent piece of work, Anstey and Bull (1989) suggest that the translation of assessment into planning and practice is dependent on

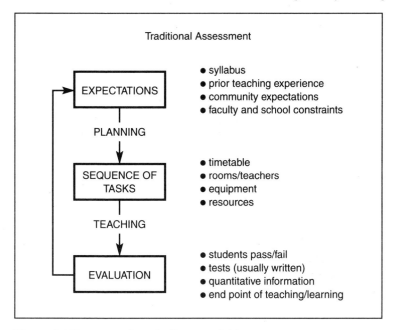

Figure 7.1 Representation of a linear model for assessment

'theoretical knowledge' (of language, learning styles, child development, culture and learning and curricula), 'practical knowledge' (of
previous teaching experience, teaching strategies, resources and
school programmes and policies) and 'particular knowledge' of children (including their knowledge and experience, interests, expectations and school and cultural environment). This, they argue, leads
to the integrated use of planning, monitoring and assessment which
ultimately leads to the translation of knowledge into practice. While
conceptually this framework is useful, it adopts a different definition
of assessment to that which is integral to this book, placing monitoring at the centre of the teaching/learning cycle.

What I am proposing is that all teaching and learning is dependent on a cycle of planning, teaching assessment and reflection. This
I have referred to as the *teaching and learning cycle*. As Figure 7.2 shows,
teaching and learning are seen as reciprocal processes that are part
of an ongoing cycle of action and reflection. Central to this cycle is
the constant assessment of student literacy and learning which informs planning, classroom practice and, ultimately, the evaluation of

137

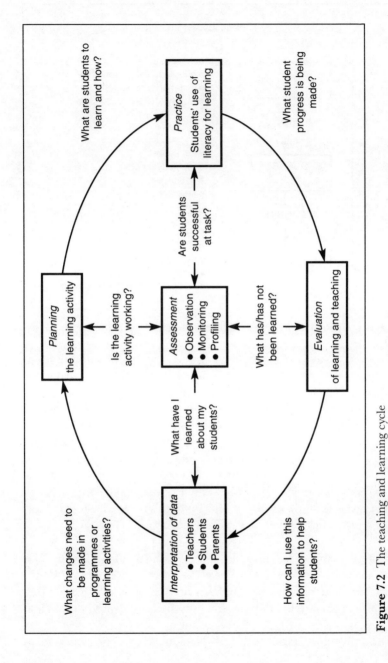

Figure 7.2 The teaching and learning cycle
(An earlier form of this diagram was developed with Rhonda Jenkins as part of an unpublished professional development package funded by the Australian Curriculum Corporation.)

student learning. This whole process is dependent on teachers who are prepared to ask questions of themselves, their students and their students' parents.

If one adopts the above framework for assessment then not surprisingly the practices that will be used to make decisions about student learning will be different from those made in classrooms where assessment is seen as part of a linear teaching sequence. In the sections that follow I describe how one uses this framework.

What do we assess?

Before a teacher embarks on assessment it is important to know what he/she is looking for. It has always been a well-known axiom that before one observes one must first know what to look for. However, before deciding what to look for, it is a good idea to re-examine our stated principles. At once it will be recognized that the 'what' will be influenced by principles concerning the multidimensional nature of data, the concern to observe 'whole' language, the need for collaboration with others, and the fact that assessments should be authentic.

A number of authors have attempted to offer simple overviews of the forms that observation can take. The following is how I see the range of observations that need to be made about literacy. It has been influenced by many teaching experiences and, no doubt, a number of publications. The South Australian Department of Education's document *Literacy Assessment in Practice* (1991) has been particularly influential.

1. VARIATIONS OF WRITTEN LANGUAGE

It is important to observe a variety of students reading, writing and talking about reading and writing. Variation should occur in:

- Text difficulty
- Text genre
- Purpose
- Audience.

2. KNOWLEDGE ABOUT LANGUAGE

It is important to assess students' knowledge of language. This is an important element of assessment for inexperienced and experienced literacy users alike. The following are some of the issues to be explored:

- Does the literacy user have knowledge of how written language works appropriate to his/her experience (e.g. concepts of print for emergent literacy user, knowledge of written genres for older students)?
- Does the literacy learner use reading and writing for a range of appropriate purposes?
- Can the literacy learner read or write a range of written genres?
- Does the literacy learner understand the use of language conventions (e.g. punctuation)?
- Can the literacy learner use language to talk about and describe written language?

3. ATTITUDES TO AND PERCEPTIONS OF LITERACY

- How does the student view him/herself as a literacy user?
- What are the student's attitudes to literacy?
- Does the student have specific interests in literacy?
- How does the student conceptualize the nature and purposes of reading and writing?

4. HOW IS LITERACY DEMONSTRATED (PRODUCT)?

Written products
- Does the writing achieve its purpose?
- Does it have originality and freshness?
- Is it focused writing?
- Does the writer show authority over topic?
- Is it well-structured?
- Has language been used well?
- Is it tight writing?
- Is the writer able to write for a variety of purposes, e.g. record, describe, clarify thinking, predict, persuade, communicate news or information, argue?
- Can the writer use a range of appropriate genres, e.g. recounts, reports, narrative, argument, exposition?

Demonstrations of reading

- Does the reader understand the purpose of the reading?
- Does the reader display good understanding of the topic, literary themes, word meanings, subtleties of characterization, author bias, etc.?

- Is the reader's meaning consistent with the text and the author's intended meaning?
- Can the reader use the appropriate reading practices to learn in a variety of contexts and for a range of purposes?

5. WHAT READING AND WRITING STRATEGIES ARE USED (PROCESS)?

- Can the writer use strategies for planning, drafting, revising and preparing writing for publication?
- Does the reader engage with the text, critique the text, reflect on the text and respond to it?
- Can the literacy user monitor and assess the effectiveness of his/ her reading and writing?
- Can the reader/writer assume the roles of codebreaker (e.g. know about sound–symbol relationships), participant (e.g. recognizing structural features of text), user (e.g. recognize the purpose of a text) and critic (e.g. detect bias, point of view, etc.) as described by Freebody and Luke (1992)?

How do we assess?

Having looked in general terms at what we assess, I now want to turn my attention to how we assess. I want to begin by stressing that observation is the principal data gathering tool of the teacher. As Yetta Goodman (1978) stressed, teachers are to be constant 'kid watchers'. Good assessment is based on close and continuous monitoring of student reading and writing of both a structured and an informal kind. As the definition at the beginning of the chapter indicates, it is the detailed and focused attention to the ways in which individuals or groups of students participate in learning tasks, and is usually recorded in the form of anecdotal records, checklists, or portfolios.

I want to provide an overview of these broad generic observation strategies and then in the next section provide some specific examples of focused observation techniques.

INTERVIEWS

The purpose of the interview is to gain an insight into the student's

- understanding of the reading and writing processes
- strategies that are consciously used for reading and writing
- use of reading and writing texts, purposes and audiences

141

Table 7.1

Sample questions	Purpose of the questions
Do you like reading? Why or why not?	Knowledge about attitude to reading.
Who is the best reader you know? What influenced your choice?	Understanding of what reading is and what is critical to the reading process.
What do you find hardest about writing?	Knowledge of the student's writing process, difficulties and needs.
What do you do when you come to a difficult word while reading?	Knowledge of strategies used in reading.
Why did you start the writing in this way? Could you have done it more effectively?	Knowledge of the writer's understanding of audience and writing style
Why did you portray the character in this way?	Understanding of extent of student skill in characterization.
How do you know when to begin and end quotation marks?	Understanding of how language works.

- attitudes to and interests in reading and writing
- metacognitive knowledge of literacy.

Interviews can be conducted in different ways, varying by participants (individual or group), purpose (e.g. information about interests, strategy use, knowledge of language) and structure (informal or formal). Table 7.1 offers a sample of questions that could be asked in an interview to gain differing knowledge about students.

JOURNALS AND LOG BOOKS

Journals or logs are essentially a record of student work and achievement. Their purpose will vary greatly depending on whether they are kept by the student or teacher, and depending on their stated purpose. The difference between a log and a journal is that the log tends to be a verbatim record of what is read and written, whereas the journal tends to be more encyclopaedic and selective. The following are some of the varied purposes for using logs and journals:

Personal reading log – the student records all personal reading, listing the title, author and date completed.

Student writing journal – the student uses a large book to keep an on-going record of ideas for writing, reflections on pieces written, feedback from readers, plans for future writing.

Student reading journal – the student uses the journal to keep written responses to literature that has been read, reflections on favourite authors, student and teacher recommendations for reading, favourite poems and lines from novels, quotable quotations, etc.

Teacher writing journal – this journal is kept by the teacher as a record of all writing set, significant developments in writing in the class (e.g. new things learned), strategies being employed (e.g. nature of conferences), reflections on own teaching.

Teacher log book – this is simply a detailed chronological record of reading and writing activities planned, significant student reactions and outcomes (especially as this relates to the effectiveness of the practice), texts read to the class, etc.

ANECDOTAL RECORDS

While anecdotal records are similar to logs and journals, the essential difference is that these records are more comprehensive, are focused on specific students, and are usually kept by the teacher. They are normally kept as part of an ongoing assessment of students in specific areas. The most common use of anecdotal records is as part of individual student profiles. For example, a teacher might keep a file on every child's writing. This would be accessed whenever the teacher has a conference with the child, after any formal assessment, when significant incidents occur that relate to the student's use of reading and writing. Anecdotal records can record student literacy in many forms. Table 7.2 provides a sample of the types of records that can be kept and their purpose.

PORTFOLIOS

Portfolios are usually used for writing, although portfolios for both reading and writing are possible. A portfolio is essentially a collection of student writing. It provides a record of the writing that a student has done throughout the year. However, some teachers and students

Table 7.2

Sample anecdotal record	Purpose of the record
'Jason had problems today with the use of apostrophes'	Record of common surface feature problems
'At last Karen has read something other than a Roald Dahl book'	Record of student reading interests
'Karl still cannot make good choices about books to read'	Record of student reading habits
'Salim still has great difficulty with report genre – everything degenerates into a recount'	Record of student difficulty with knowledge of written genres
'Holley seems to over-rely on decoding when reading – miscues tend to be semantically incorrect, and she doesn't self-correct'	Record of student's reading strategies
'Joanne has lost all confidence in her ability to read – she needs easier texts for a while'	Record of student attitudes to reading and specific needs in text choice
'Rolf asked some wonderful questions in the group writing conferences today'	Record of student progress in monitoring of own language and ability to share this with others

add other material to the portfolio. This includes personal spelling lists, topic lists, reader feedback, teacher observations of specific pieces of writing, checklists relating to writing conventions, etc. The way in which portfolios are compiled also varies from weekly updates by the student to regular monthly updates which are linked with school-based assessments and communication with parents. Given the importance of portfolios, they will be discussed in greater detail later in this chapter.

DEVELOPMENTAL CHECKLISTS

Checklists are also used commonly for both reading and writing. The checklist is both a guide for teacher observation and a means to aid student self-assessment. Typically the checklist has a list of literacy practices and skills that it is assumed children at specific stages of development need to demonstrate. Common uses include:

Recording the development of revision and editing skills
Monitoring the development of graphophonic knowledge
Recording of students' comprehension ability
Monitoring spelling ability
Recording student knowledge of concepts of print.

OBSERVATIONS OF READING AND WRITING OUTCOMES

One of the most common forms of assessment includes the direct observation and recording of data concerning the writing produced or the reading demonstrated by students. This usually involves some form of analysis of the written products.

Writing

The major way in which writing is assessed is through the application of one or more sets of criteria to assess writing samples. At times this can be supplemented by the use of checklists and holistic scoring. The latter usually involves the teacher (or peers) reading the piece and giving it an overall score (on a specific scale, such as 1 to 10) or specific scores relating to different criteria. The criteria that are recommended for this purpose have already been outlined above and are guided by the following questions:

Does the writing achieve its purpose?
Does it have originality and freshness?
Is it focused writing?
Does the writer show authority over topic?
Is it well-structured?
Has language been used well?
Is it tight writing?

Assessment over time usually involves the analysis of a number of pieces of writing paying attention to the need to sample specific genres, as well as different purposes and audiences for writing. This process is at times linked with portfolios, with students (particularly older students) presenting the teacher with a diverse set of writing for assessment.

Reading

Reading is also assessed through direct observations of the products of reading. This includes the use of the following procedures:

Cloze passages to assess comprehension
Written responses to reading (particularly literature)
Reading tests of comprehension, word knowledge and vocabulary
Retelling analysis.

OBSERVATIONS OF READING AND WRITING PROCESSES

By far the most difficult form of assessment is analysis of the reading and writing processes. This usually requires a combination of observation, interviews and the monitoring of reading and writing behaviours. Table 7.3 outlines some of the most common ways in which this is done.

Table 7.3

Observations made	Purpose of the observation
Student comments made during draft writing	These provide an insight into the nature of the writing strategies being used and the decisions being made during writing
The types of questions students ask of other students during conferences	This provides an insight into the students' knowledge of revision and the features of 'quality' writing
Observation of reading miscues	This provides evidence of the mental processing of text and the type of cueing strategies being employed
Analysis of reader responses	These provide an insight into the mental texts the reader is constructing
Think-alouds	This verbal running record of what the reader was thinking at specific points in the text provides information on the meaning making that is occurring
Error analysis of writing	This provides an insight into the spelling strategies of writers

An example of one teacher's focused assessment strategies

The following example is provided to show how the assessment in one class is constructed to use a variety of assessment strategies to monitor literacy development. The teacher has a grade 4 class (age approximately 9 years) and is attempting to provide a balanced assessment of each child's development and progress as well as providing an insight into the effectiveness of the teaching strategies being used. Table 7.4 provides an overview of the strategies used.

Table 7.4

Strategy	Form of data	Purpose	Comments
READING			
Cloze procedure	Completed Cloze sheets	Provide information on comprehension	Administered using a variety of text types approximately four times per year
Miscue analysis	Record of miscues for specific texts analysed by type (i.e. semantic, syntactic and graphophonic)	Provides information on nature of students' reading processes	Administered at least four times per year
Retelling analysis	Written verbatim retelling analysed for presence of major text elements and overall gist of text	Assessment of comprehension and text processing strategies	Administered four times per year
Record of reading	Student kept record of all independent reading	Indicator of depth and diversity of student reading	Progress also monitored through reading conferences
Reading interviews	Verbatim record of student response to specific questions	Insight into attitude to reading, reading interests, reading strategies	Administered twice per year
Anecdotal records	Written comments recorded by the teacher	Record of student problems, strengths, new learning, attitudes, interests …	Continuous record maintained weekly

Table 7.4 (cont.)

Strategy	Form of data	Purpose	Comments
WRITING PORTFOLIO (all assessment is based on the portfolio)			
Running record of writing	One week's writing each month including draft and published work	Provides a sense of the student's writing output including variety of genres, purposes and audiences	This writing can also be sent home to parents with a a covering letter
Selected writing	Monthly selection of specific pieces of writing including at least three different genres and writing purposes	Indicator of the quality of the writing produced allowing individual and class judgements of development	Can be used for individual or group assessments
Complete record of all writing	List of all pieces of writing completed during the year	Simple overview of writing which permits analysis of topics, genres, completion	Record kept by student
Writing revision strategies	Record of revision foci evident in personal editing checklists – built up over the year	Record of growth and needs in revision as well as basis for discussion at conferences	Kept by students in their writing folders. Additional anecdotal records kept by teacher
Spelling progress	Record of personal spelling progress	Indicator of progress and needs	Kept by students in writing folders. Additional anecdotal records kept by teacher
Holistic scoring	Writing assessment sheet that consists of a series of holistic scores on each of the writing criteria outlined above	Provides students with an assessment of their best piece of writing	Students select their best piece of writing. Used for evaluation purposes also

What should be noticed about the above teacher's assessment overview is that it conforms closely to the framework outlined earlier in this chapter. It utilizes frequent observation of student reading and writing from multiple perspectives. In addition, it involves students closely in this assessment process and provides an avenue for feedback to parents. The diversity of observations made also allows the teacher to plan and revise teaching to accommodate student needs. An important part of this process is the teacher's reflection on these data, which ultimately leads to action in the form of student support or modifications to teaching.

Alternative approaches to assessment

While the above has provided an overview of commonly used approaches to assessment I want to challenge you the reader to constantly seek alternative approaches to assessment that are consistent with the principles I have outlined as well as the framework that has been described. As a teacher I am constantly seeking more effective and more authentic ways to assess the learning of my students. Let me discuss several areas where my explorations have only just begun but which I believe offer us great potential.

STUDENT SELF-ASSESSMENT

Student self-assessment is ultimately the key to student learning. It is only when we begin to monitor our own learning that significant progress occurs in learning. While assessment can always be something that someone 'does to someone else' this wastes the valuable potential that self-assessment has for learning. As the discussion in the rest of this chapter has shown, student involvement in assessment is relatively easy to achieve. The following are some of the ways in which it can be achieved:

Involve students in the compilation of portfolios.

Seek students' opinions about their best work (and ask them why they think as they do).

Ask students to keep records of their reading and writing.

Have students monitor their revision strategies using an individual checklist kept in their writing folders.

Have students monitor their spelling, punctuation and grammar as part of the editing of writing.

Ask students to analyse their reading habits using their reading records.

Ask students to record student comments on their writing as part of a group conference.

149

It is important to note that each of the above suggestions involves the students in the collection and interpretation of data. The purpose of self-assessment is to allow students to develop a better understanding of their literacy strengths, weaknesses and needs. This allows them to seek support from the teacher and other peers and to set themselves new goals for learning.

PARENT INVOLVEMENT

There is great potential for the involvement of parents in the assessment processes of our students. The major purposes of this strategy are to:

- provide parents with more complete information on their children's literacy
- offer a means for parents and children to talk about school work
- enlist the support of parents in the monitoring of student progress in literacy.

Parents can be involved in a number of ways, ranging from simple observation of their work and acknowledgement by way of signature to participation in their children's reading and writing.

Portfolios

One effective way to involve parents is through the use of portfolios. While at times simply sending home students' school books is useful, a more systematic approach to the sharing of student work is preferable. One procedure for using literacy portfolios developed by Cairney and Munsie (1992b) follows.

Step 1: Prepare a list of literacy work to be taken home. This might include:

- Several examples of narrative writing. This should include draft materials as well as the final product.
- Samples of writing from other subjects, e.g. a report from science, notes made on a video, an excursion assignment.
- A list of frequently misspelt words.
- A text that the child has chosen to read to his/her parents.
- A list of books read up to this point in time. Such a list might include the title, author and date completed.
- A self-evaluation prepared by the child.

Step 2: Prepare the portfolios with each child's involvement. Explain the purpose of the work sample to the students.

Step 3: Send the work sample home with its purpose outlined as well as procedures for parents to follow up any of the material included (Figure 7.3).

Step 4: Provide time for parents to visit the school to discuss the work sample.

While parental involvement in portfolio use might begin in this way, it would be possible in time to involve parents more fully by seeking their views on their child's progress and areas where they see improvement, strengths and needs.

Dear Parent,

Attached is a sample of your child's literacy work in the past four weeks. The sample includes:

- Two stories (draft and published work).

- Three pieces of writing from other subjects.

- A list of words that your child needs help with.

- A book which they will read to you.

- A list of books read in the last four weeks.

The purpose of the work sample is to keep you informed about the work your child is completing and to help you to gauge progress.

Please use the sample as an opportunity to praise your child's efforts. You might also use it to offer help where problems are evident.

If you have any questions about the work sample or your child's progress please let me know.

Sincerely,

Figure 7.3 Sample letter to parents outlining the purpose of portfolios

Paired Reading

Another good way to involve parents in assessing their children's literacy is through listening to their children read at home. A common technique for this purpose is Paired Reading. This simple technique was first designed by Morgan (1976) and was later refined by Topping and McKnight (1984), and Topping and Wolfendale (1985). It involves two phases. The first is a simultaneous phase where a tutor and child sit next to each other reading out loud together. The tutor adjusts the reading speed to that of the child. Miscues are picked up as the reading proceeds, the child being asked to repeat the correct word before proceeding.

The second independent reading phase involves a similar pattern of synchronized reading, except the reader attempts independent reading when confident. This is achieved by encouraging the child to gently tap the tutor when he/she feels that it is possible to read independently. The tutor praises the child and he/she proceeds until an error is made. This is then corrected by the tutor reading the original version. The reading then proceeds in a synchronized way until the child again signals to the tutor for independent reading to begin.

Cairney and Munsie (1992b) suggest that a good way to introduce this strategy is to invite parents to the classroom to take part in a Paired Reading session. Prior to the session, provide a description of the Paired Reading technique for parents (see Figure 7.4, from Cairney and Munsie, 1992b). When the visit occurs, allow parents to first observe the technique being used (by you the teacher) with a child. At the end of this demonstration, allow time for them to ask questions about the technique and its benefits. Following this discussion, have all parents try the technique with their children.

The ongoing use of this technique can be easily extended once it has been commenced to include the recording of observations about their children's reading. For example, parents could be asked to complete a modified form of running record, focusing on the rate of miscues and their type. Parents might also be asked to record instances of self-correction, use of illustrations, specific difficulties, reading interests and the level of comprehension evidenced by discussion. When paired reading is used in this way it is necessary to provide parent workshops on the techniques before proceeding.

PAIRED READING

This is a simple method for reading with your child. It has been shown to be an effective way to help children develop as readers. When using it follow the following steps:

Step 1   Ask your child to choose a book that they would like to read.

Step 2   Explain that you're going to do some Paired Reading.

Step 3   Sit alongside your child with them holding the book. Point out to your child that you are going to read the book out loud with them following.

Step 4   Begin reading adjusting your pace to suit your child. Words that are missed by the child are repeated by them in correct form, then they read on.

    Read for 5–10 minutes per day.

Step 5   After confidence has been achieved with the above (1 to 3 weeks) introduce the second stage of Paired Reading.

    This is similar to the first stage except the reader attempts to read alone when confident. Begin reading together but encourage your child to tap you when they wish to read alone. You praise the child, then he/she reads till a miscue is made. This is corrected and both read on till the child again feels confident to read alone.

Step 6   Increase periods of reading up to 15 minutes.

Step 7   Stop using this technique when the child becomes bored with it or when progress is so great that it is no longer needed.

Figure 7.4 Sample outline of the Paired Reading technique prepared for parents

Using editing checklists
Another way to involve parents is through the use of editing check-lists. As suggested already, this is one effective way to focus student attention on specific aspects of revision. Parent help can be enlisted in this process.

Before asking parents to help their children to use an editing checklist, invite them either to an in-school writing lesson or to an after-school parent session focusing on writing. The best way to conduct such a demonstration is to use a piece of your own writing on an overhead projector and an editing checklist that you have designed for the purposes of the demonstration.

Following this demonstration, parents should sit with their children and help them to work through their own piece of writing using an editing checklist that you have provided (see Figure 7.5 for an example). After this session parents can be encouraged to help their children to use similar procedures at home. This could be followed up 3–4 weeks later with an after-school session at which parents could be asked about the process that has been used. If checklists are used in this way it is important for their purpose to be made clear to all parents. What needs to be stressed is that the checklist is a tool for assisting self-revision, not a test to find out what is wrong with draft writing.

- Have I used a logical sequence of ideas or facts?

- Does the piece start in such a way that the reader will want to read on?

- Check sentence beginnings. Have I varied them?

- Have I used commas in the right places?

- Has paragraphing been used?

- Use your list of common spelling errors to check your work.

- Read it out loud to someone else.

Figure 7.5 Sample editing checklist

Alternative strategies to assess reading comprehension

Like Valencia and Pearson (1987), I want to argue that if reading and writing are going to be properly assessed, strategies are required which provide access to this process of meaning making, not simply whether information has been transferred or reproduced. One particular area of need is the use of questions in different ways. As I pointed out in Chapter 5, questions have often been used in a restricted way simply to test knowledge. This restricted use of questions is designed to narrow a student's focus to a single meaning, whereas our aim should be to use questions to get at multiple meanings (Cairney, 1990a, 1990b).

A problem with the strategies that have been used previously to assess reading comprehension is that they fail to recognize the critical relationship that should exist between teaching and assessment. In recent years I have been exploring alternative strategies that attempt to sample a wider cross-section of the meanings that readers are constructing as part of the reading process. These alternative strategies also bring together what should be the complementary and interdependent processes of assessment and teaching of reading comprehension.

The following are several strategies that I have been using to attempt to gain a greater insight into the nature of the reading process in order to make better decisions about teaching. Each of these has been developed as an outgrowth of comprehension research (see Cairney, 1986, 1990a, 1990b) exploring the use of alternative modes for heightening student engagement with text.

STORY MAPPING

Story mapping is a simple strategy that requires students to draw a pictorial representation of a setting for a narrative text (Cairney, 1990a). Students are asked to imagine the setting (or part of the setting) for a particular story and to produce a representation of it as it would appear from the air (Figure 7.6). In asking the reader to draw the physical setting of the narrative text the teacher gains an insight into the students' ability to engage in imaging and also their understanding of the setting as described by the author.

Figure 7.6 An example of story mapping (Roald Dahl, *Boy*)

SKETCH TO STRETCH

Sketch to Stretch also uses drawing, but is linked closely with text prediction and imagery (Harste *et al.*, 1985; Cairney, 1990a). At specific points within a narrative text students are asked to produce a sketch which represents what they think will happen next, what has just taken place, or how they visualize a particular event or character (Figure 7.7). Sketch to Stretch is a powerful way to gain an insight into the mental texts that students are constructing as well as their engagement with text.

CHARACTER RATING SCALES

Character rating scales represent an instructional strategy which was first developed by Johnson and Louis (1985). This strategy requires students to make judgements about characters in accordance with a series of personality traits (Cairney, 1990a), for example intelligence, kindness or aggressiveness (see Figure 7.8). Students are either given

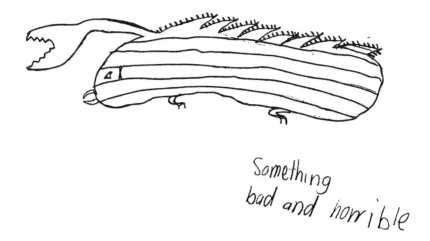

Figure 7.7 An example of Sketch to Stretch

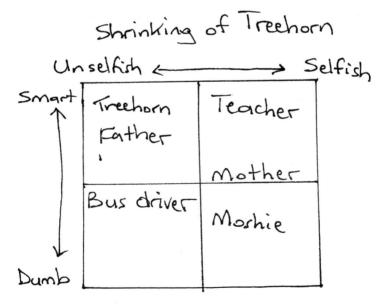

Figure 7.8 An example of a character rating scale

JAWS A BAD INFLUENCE

Fear of sharks has increased in recent years because of the films *Jaws*, *Jaws II*, and *Blue Water*, *White Death*. After seeing *Jaws*, some people have declared that they would never swim in the sea again. In these shark horror movies the creatures are portrayed as vicious man-eaters. South Australian shark expert, Mr Rodney Fox, says that the white pointer has been unjustly given a bad name by these films. "Few people have been attacked by sharks. The fear of the white pointer has been multiplied out of all proportion. Off our shores we have many sharks, and if it were true about the white pointer, the beaches would provide a smorgasbord for them every weekend," Mr Fox told a reporter.

← You bet!

Wouldn't say horor

Rubbish

I like this

He said that white pointers do not bite objects but they "mouth" them. Because sharks cannot see well, they use this method to discover whether or not an object is food. This is why the sharks seem to attack boats' rudders or the metal cages which protect divers.

I'm not going be there dinner

However, Mr Fox does not believe that sharks are harmless creatures. He was badly injured when attacked by a white pointer in 1963. His advice is that if you see a shark when you are swimming, don't panic. You should swim slowly away from it while trying to keep the shark in view. "Most attacks have been from behind," he said.

Scream and yell — that's what I'd do

SHARKS ON CAMERA

Mr Fox organises expeditions in the waters around Port Lincoln, South Australia. This area has many large white pointers. Metal cages are hung from a boat. Divers enter these cages and from there can film the big sharks in safety. The sharks are attracted to the boats by pieces of fish and meat thrown overboard.

Good move

The sharks move effortlessly through the water. They will swim right up to the cage and push it around. The diver inside gets a close-up view of the shark's teeth. This can be quite a sight! When a shark opens its jaw, the lower jawbone is thrust forward while the snout is drawn back and up, until it makes almost a right angle with the shark's body. At this moment, the mouth is located forward of the head, and no longer beneath it. It resembles a large wolf trap, equipped with many sharp, gleaming teeth. A large shark would easily have the strength to tear a cage to pieces if it wanted to.

?

They bite

Figure 7.9 An example of Talk to the Author

the traits or are asked to suggest them. They then provide a rating of specific characters using a sliding scale that represents each personality trait. This strategy provides information on students' understanding of characterization as well as on their overall understanding of the relationship between characters, something that requires a grasp of the 'gist' of the text.

TALK TO THE AUTHOR

This strategy was initially developed simply as a teaching device (Cairney, 1986, 1990b), but recently I have been exploring its use as an assessment device. Essentially it involves a written dialogue between a reader and the implied author (Figure 7.9). Readers are encouraged to ask questions of the author, disagree with him/her, seek clarification, offer opinions, add extra information. This strategy can be used with either narrative or factual texts. The great advantage of this strategy is that it provides a window into the reading process. Through the comments and questions students ask you can gain an insight into the text that they are constructing, the background knowledge that is being primed, and the intertextual connections that are being made as they read.

Conclusion

The purpose of this chapter has been to provide an overview of assessment and to argue for its integration into the teaching and learning process. The ideas and strategies have been influenced by the principles outlined at the start of the chapter and also by the framework that has been developed. Assessment is obviously integral to all that we do as teachers of literacy, but it must never divert attention away from the 'main game', that is, students' engagement in meaning making that relates to purposes for learning that are relevant to them and which ultimately equips them for learning.

Assessment is thus critical both for learning and for the planning of teaching programmes that facilitate learning. The purpose of Chapter 8 will be to demonstrate how good assessment links to the planning of effective programmes for literacy.

CHAPTER 8

Programming for literacy instruction

Introduction

When I first began teaching, one of the greatest chores I faced was the programme I had to write each term. When I look back on this time, and reflect on why it was such a drudgery, I think the answer is that the programme was something that was primarily written for my supervisor. It was in a format that he had decided, it was handed in on a day that he decided, and it was critiqued on his terms. In addition, the content was controlled fairly closely by a series of syllabuses. To top it all off, the programming was reflective of an approach which was largely linear, and which was very much consistent with the assessment model outlined at the start of Chapter 7. Thankfully, my experiences with my grade 6 class and the literature programme broke this cycle.

As my instructional model changed from one that was teacher-centred to one that was geared to develop a community of learners, so too did my approach to programming. With the change in instructional model came a new perspective on assessment and teaching which was more closely aligned with the Teaching and Learning Cycle outlined in Chapter 7. It was the assumptions that are foundational to this cycle that began to influence my programme development.

It is important to restate these assumptions before discussing programming more fully:

- Assessment should be based on the observation of 'whole' language (i.e. fully contextualized language) in action.
- Assessment and evaluation are an integral part of the teaching and learning cycle.
- Assessment should be continuous.
- Assessment and evaluation should be multidimensional.
- Assessment should be collaborative (i.e. informed by others).

- Assessment and evaluation should be grounded in knowledge of literacy.
- Assessment and evaluation should be authentic.
- Assessment and evaluation should inform students and lead to new directions in teaching.

Programming is in essence the recording of one's teaching and learning plans. There is little consensus among teachers concerning the best approach to programming. This is quite acceptable, because programming is a highly individualized process which must match the teacher's strengths, teaching style and needs. Nevertheless, there are broad issues and concerns that all teachers face when considering programming. I will examine these issues before looking more closely at programming approaches.

Common issues and concerns

The first issue to confront all primary school teachers when faced with programming is whether to pre-programme everything or allow some aspects of the programme to be recorded retrospectively. This may seem a trivial issue, but it is important, and has a strong influence on the approach to programming.

Often school administrators insist on complete pre-programming. While in principle this seems a reasonable request (the need for proper planning is a truism), if one adopts an approach to teaching that consists of a cycle of planning, teaching, assessment, evaluation and reflection then one must be open to changes to the teaching programme and be prepared to make constant adjustments to meet the changing needs of learners. Because of this, it is my view that a completely pre-planned programme is restrictive. As a result, I tend to use a combination of pre- and retrospective programming.

A second issue is the form that programmes will take. Some teachers prefer to use a bound book which is suitably ruled into boxes or columns to enable information to be categorized in specific ways. Some teachers even design their own programme template with consistent headings (e.g. outcomes, content, teaching strategies, assessment). It is important to stress that there is no best format for programming; teachers should develop their own style that suits their needs.

Steps to programming

In spite of the diversity that is possible in programming approaches, I want to suggest that there are a number of common steps to programming that most teachers follow. The following sequence of steps is based on one first developed by Cairney (1983/1990). Each step will be described in detail.

STEP 1: ASSESSMENT OF NEEDS

Needs assessment begins as soon as a teacher enters the classroom on the first day of school. As described in Chapter 7, this assessment takes many forms and is ongoing. Most assessment is done at an informal level and is dependent on observation. The teacher begins from day one noting individual and class strengths, weaknesses and needs. Typically, anecdotal records are kept, and analyses of student interviews, reading and writing products and processes are made. In addition, details concerning previous programmes are gleaned from school records, and previous teachers are consulted. Initial meetings may be held with parents to determine their expectations, and to gain a different perspective on the child and his/her school experience. This preliminary observation usually covers the broad areas identified in Chapter 7 and utilizes a range of assessment strategies.

STEP 2: ESTABLISH PRIORITIES FOR TEACHING AND LEARNING

Once the initial assessment of students has occurred, a number of expected outcomes are set. In addition, I normally prepare a rationale for my programme which makes clear my assumptions about literacy and learning. The expected outcomes normally include those set for the class (e.g. to increase the number of books read independently, to improve basic research skills, etc.) and those focused on specific students with special needs (e.g. to help Craig rely less upon graphophonic information when reading in order to increase his utilization of other strategies). These goals will be influenced by a number of factors external to the teacher, including syllabus requirements, school policies and procedures in particular areas, available resources, and the teacher's strengths and teaching style.

STEP 3: MAKE DECISIONS CONCERNING THE PROGRAMME COMPONENTS

Once the expected outcomes are selected it is necessary to decide what emphases will be adopted with your class. For example, if your children seem to have little interest in reading, an independent reading programme will be of critical importance. On the other hand, if your students are keen readers, but rarely use reading to learn, a strong research component will be essential. While the components may be similar from class to class the relative balance will vary. They may also vary across the year.

In most programmes the following components are covered in reading and writing:

Reading – silent independent reading, teacher 'read alouds' of literature, group discussion of common texts that have been read (both literary and factual), reading for a variety of purposes (e.g. oral reading, study skills, etc.), comprehension (typically involving strategies to heighten engagement with texts), opportunities for response to reading, shared reading (e.g. reading 'Big Books', Language Experience strategies, etc.), and word study (usually integrated within the preceding components but including focused activities for those students who need it).

Writing – some form of writing workshop, writing across the curriculum (e.g. science, art, mathematics), strategies for revision (e.g. conferences, mini-lessons), knowledge of language (e.g. discussion of genres, grammar, punctuation and spelling).

How teachers decide upon the relative emphasis on each component will depend on the needs of the children.

STEP 4: ORGANIZATION OF THE CLASSROOM RESOURCES

The selection of resources is normally closely integrated with all of the above steps rather than occurring as a separate step. Existing school resources are assessed, the library examined, and community resources evaluated. Inevitably, the available resources influence the programme planned. However, the limitation of reading and writing resources should never prevent the planning of an effective programme as long as library resources are available.

STEP 5: DETERMINE THE OVERALL PROGRAMMING APPROACH

The overall programming approach will have a major effect upon the teaching and learning activities planned. While many of the literacy activities that will be planned in any classroom are part of other subjects, there will always be a core literacy programme in any primary classroom. It is within this core literacy programme that a great deal of literacy development takes place. The approach that is adopted in this core component will have a significant effect on the way the programme is planned. For example, if the decision is made to use a literature-based approach as the core of the literacy programme, the specific lessons planned will vary greatly from a programme which might (for example) be based on an integrated reading scheme.

STEP 6: PLAN THE PROGRAMME CONTENT

Once the framework is decided, the next step is to plan appropriate teaching and learning strategies and to put in place procedures for enabling students to use reading and writing for a range of purposes. There are two major components to this planning. First, there are procedural plans to be made. For example, you now need to decide how the writing workshop and independent reading will be set up in your classroom. What procedures will be followed, how often will students write, how will revision strategies be supported (e.g. use of conferences, checklists, etc.)? Will you use a structured Drop Everything and Read (DEAR) programme for independent reading, or a less formally arranged programme? Second, you need to plan specific literacy activities that relate to focused expected outcomes in components of literacy such as comprehension, spelling, writing revision strategies, etc.

STEP 7: DECIDE HOW YOU WILL ASSESS PROGRESS IN LITERACY AND WHAT RECORDS WILL BE KEPT

The next component of planning is to decide how student progress will be assessed and recorded. This is closely integrated with step 6. As programme components are planned (even the procedural components like DEAR), the decisions concerning how progress is to be assessed must be made. At a global level, key decisions will need to be made about procedures for gathering data on student literacy (e.g. will I use portfolios? will I ask students to keep personal reading records?). At a more specific learner level, decisions will need to be made about the assessment strategies to be used, their frequency, who is to implement them and so on.

This step is obviously closely related to the previous one. It is assessment data that enable the teacher to evaluate the effectiveness of the programme planned. This is done by analysing the assessment data collected, looking for trends and for evidence that the original goals and the expected outcomes of the programme have been met.

Are my students making satisfactory progress in all areas of literacy?

Are my students using literacy for a range of purposes related to learning?

Are my students enjoying school and developing in confidence and self-esteem?

Are my students developing positive attitudes towards reading and writing?

Are my students growing in their knowledge of written language and how it is used?

A generic programme framework

It is virtually impossible to outline an authentic example of a class programme in a book of this type. However, what is possible is to provide a framework that all primary school teachers might find useful. I will describe this framework and provide examples throughout to give an indication of how a programme might be developed. I believe that a programme should have the following key sections:

- Programme rationale
- An outline of key outcomes that form part of your programme
- A description of generic or procedural components of your programme
- An outline of specific teaching and learning strategies
- Details on assessment
- A resources section.

I will now describe each of these components of the framework in detail.

PROGRAMME RATIONALE

This section of your programme should be a short outline (one to three typed pages) of your beliefs about literacy, learning and teaching. This will normally state clearly how you believe literacy is learned and what your role as teacher is in fostering this development. It would then be followed by a statement that summarizes your views on the key values, attitudes, skills and knowledge that you see as needing to be developed. This statement will reflect what you have learned in pre-service and in-service teacher education programmes, key syllabus and curriculum documents, and teachers' reference books like the one you are reading.

Sample Programme Rationale

Literacy is both a cognitive and a sociocultural process. One learns about literacy within a social context, as an extension of relationships with other people. Hence, the meanings we create as we read and write are always relative. The meanings we make can never be removed from the social context within which we create them. As James Gee expresses it, we learn to read and write by 'being apprenticed to a social group'.

The meanings we construct as we read and write reflect who we are, what we have experienced, what we know about language and the world, and also our purposes for creating them in the first place.

Reading and writing are both constructive processes that require us to make meaning. In summary:

- Reading and writing are cultural practices. Neither reading nor writing are unitary skills. Rather, they are sets of practices that serve social functions.
- Readers and writers create meaning, they don't simply transcribe, summarize or extract it.
- The meaning readers and writers create is always 'greater' than the written text's potential meaning and the literacy user's prior knowledge and experiences.
- No two readers or writers can ever read or write the same text in the same way; nor do they arrive at the same meaning as part of these processes.

- Above all, meaning is relative, socially constructed, and must be interpreted within the context of the social purposes and relationships to which the reading or writing is directed.

As Shirley Brice Heath demonstrated, what counts as literacy is intertwined with culture. James Gee claims that literacy is 'part of the very texture of wider practices that involve talk, interaction, values and beliefs'.

All of this makes a difference to the way literacy is defined and used in my classroom, and the role that I assume as a teacher. My aim is to introduce my students to the literacy practices that they need to take their place in this world. I want them to be able to use literacy to learn, to survive, to seek pleasure, to gain employment, and to maintain relationships. To do this I will provide varied opportunities for them to encounter a range of literacy practices and to use them for a range of authentic purposes. The programme that follows outlines how I hope to achieve this major goal.

AN OUTLINE OF KEY OUTCOMES THAT FORM PART OF YOUR PROGRAMME

In this component of the programme you will outline major outcomes or attainment targets in each of the major components of literacy. While these major components may be devised by the individual teacher, they may also be set for you by the school, a syllabus, or a national curriculum statement (depending on the teaching authority for whom you work), or curriculum profiles. For example, in England teachers will probably use the components talking and listening, reading and writing, with specific attainments from the National Curriculum which reflect the age and developmental level of the students.

A DESCRIPTION OF GENERIC OR PROCEDURAL COMPONENTS OF YOUR PROGRAMME

In this section of the programme the teacher includes classroom procedures and generic components that are broadly linked to a number of outcomes or attainments. For example, descriptions of independent reading programmes (e.g. Drop Everything and Read – DEAR), the procedures used for organizing a writing workshop (see Chapter 6), generic spelling strategies (e.g. personal spelling dictionaries), a description of procedures for encouraging response to literature (see Chapter 5), a read aloud programme and so on.

As well as outlining the above more generic strategies, many teachers also describe specific procedures in detail. Usually, this is done for a term or sometimes to cover the whole year. The following procedures are typical of those that might be included here:

- Procedures for implementing co-operative learning strategies

---

Sample Co-operative Learning Procedures

Co-operative learning groups will regularly be used in this classroom. Usually these roles are assigned. Over time all students are given the opportunity to fill all roles.

Group type: Four-member friendship groups.

Group roles:

When such groups are used the following roles are assigned:

Organizer – This member tries to keep the group on task. They remind the group of time constraints and the original focus of the task.

Recorder – One member who records information for the group in accordance with the task requirements.

Summarizer – This person is required to turn the group's notes into a cohesive piece of writing consistent with the requirements of the task.

Encourager – This member's role is to focus on encouraging group members to contribute to the discussion.

Group reflection and feedback:
At the end of the group task each member contributes to an assessment of the group's effectiveness by discussing the co-operation of members, the success in using the skills, the group outcome.

- Grouping procedures used in specific subjects.
- Outline of the procedures adopted as part of a specialist element within the programme (e.g. use of the library).
- The format adopted for a block literacy programme segment.

A sample block writing lesson format for grade 1

In the block writing time set four days per week the following format will be used:

Lesson introduction (10 minutes):
Most lessons will begin with either a mini-lesson designed to outline procedures (e.g. asking questions in conferences); the celebration of one student's publication of some writing; a teacher read aloud of a specific text (often but not always literature); recap of a previous literacy lesson; or group sharing of recently read books.

Writing (20 minutes):
Most students will write for 20 minutes in each lesson. Not all students will write at the same time due to their involvement in several other possible activities (including the following).

Conferences (20 minutes devoted to this):
During the writing lesson the teacher will conduct individual conferences with a number of students (all students have a conference each week).

Writing mini-lesson (10 minutes):
In every writing lesson a specific mini-lesson will be conducted. This will normally focus on some aspect of writing related to students needs. This may be conducted in groups or as a whole class. This may involve Joint Construction of Texts.

- Procedures for dealing with specialist help for students with specific learning needs.

AN OUTLINE OF SPECIFIC TEACHING AND LEARNING STRATEGIES

This is the largest section of the programme and the component that details specific activities which are (normally) linked to the outcomes or attainments outlined earlier.

There are many possible formats for recording the details of your programme in this section. Sometimes teachers will provide an overview of the key outcomes first and follow this with a variety of strategies designed to ensure that these outcomes are achieved. While the assessment of whether these outcomes have been attained can be done individually, the programme does not include strategies linked with every outcome. This is particularly useful in some aspects of literacy where a specific strategy may well be designed to encourage the attainment of more than one outcome simultaneously (a frequent occurrence in most classrooms).

The following section from a grade 4 programme illustrates the form that this might take. This section of the programme describes a major component of reading. It is based on the NSW English Syllabus which incorporates the Australian National Profiles.

Sample programme segment for reading
Class: grade 4
Duration: four weeks
Text type: literary narrative

Related syllabus outcomes
Please note: based on NSW English K-6 Syllabus
Students will:

- Read independently using self-correction strategies such as reading on, referring back, sounding out, using textual knowledge, and using contextual knowledge.
- Interpret and discuss relationships between ideas, information and events in written texts.
- Identify and use the linguistic structures and features characteristic of a range of text types to construct meaning.

Strategies that will form the focus for this programme segment
The following strategies will form the focus of this programme:

- exploring stereotypes in texts, particularly those that are gender and character based.
- making comparisons between the world of the text and their own lives.
- exploring the major themes explored by the author in the piece of literature studied.

- considering strategies that the author uses for the development of characterization.

Programme content

This four-week programme segment will require all students to have access to a copy of Betsy Byars's book *The Pinballs* (Bodley Head, 1977). This does not represent the entire reading programme, rather it is simply the shared text component. Other components of the programme include independent reading, a teacher-read piece of literature, and research reading as part of other subjects (such as Science and Technology and Human Society and its Environment).

The following lessons will be given:

Lesson 1

Begin the lesson by distributing copies of *The Pinballs*. Provide background information on Betsy Byars and ask students to indicate books by her that have been read. Seek their views on any books that they know. Ask them to discuss in groups of three why this book might be called *The Pinballs*. Ask them to read the first section of the book and then to meet in groups of three once again to reconsider this question. Have their views changed? If so, why?

Lesson 2

Have them read the next two sections of the novel without comment. At the end of the reading form groups of five students and ask each group to use character rating scales to rate each of the characters introduced up to this point according to the following characteristics:

- intelligence versus unintelligence
- considerateness versus inconsiderateness
- patience versus lack of patience
- reliability versus unreliability.

Note: Rating scales are simply a series of one line continua with the opposite characteristics at different ends of the line (see Cairney, 1990a, 1990b). Each group places each character at a position on the line; a decision that is made on the basis of group consensus.

Have the groups report back to the class outlining why they made the decisions that they did.

Lesson 3

Ask the students to read up to the end of the fifth segment of the novel. At the end of the reading ask the class (as a whole) to discuss the question:

What type of person do you think Byars tries to portray Carlie as? How does she do this? Do you agree with her perspective?

Have the class read segment 6 of the book then form into groups of five to discuss Carlie's statement on page 24 of the book that 'they are just like pinballs'. What do you now think Carlie means? How accurate is her description? Point out to the class that this is an example of a simile. Explain what a simile is and have them think of personal examples.

Lesson 4

Have the class read up to the end of segment 11 of the book. Ask them in groups to consider the way Byars has developed the major characters in this story. Suggest that they consider how their characteristics are related to gender, or in fact appear to break gender stereotypes (Carlie is an interesting character in this respect). Have the groups list the characteristics of two major characters which they see as consistent with unjustified gender based stereotypes, and those that appear to run counter to stereotypes. Have all groups report back to the class providing justification for their responses.

Lesson 5

Read the next segment of the book and focus the class attention on Harvey's habit of writing lists. Discuss the possible use of the lists. Have the students write their own lists. Have each student share their list with another student of their choice outlining why they chose the list that they did.

Have the students read up to the end of segment 14 of the book. Ask all students to attempt one of the following written response activities:

- Write a personal diary entry that Harvey might have written on the night after he discovered the magazine with his mother's picture in it.

172

- Write a personal diary entry for Thomas J. which relates to his feelings as he watches the Benson twins 'dying'.
- Write a diary entry for Carlie at this stage of her developing relationship with the other children, focusing in particular on her views on each of them.

Lesson 6

Have the class read up to the end of segment 18 of the novel. As a class discuss the following question:

How do the personalities and problems of each of the children in this book reflect the lives that they have had? As a follow-up to this, ask the class to break into groups of five and address the question:

What do you believe is the author's view on the parents of the children in this book? How do you know? Are these views justified?

Lesson 7

Complete the reading of the rest of the book. Ask the class to break into groups of five and complete character rating scales for the same characteristics addressed in the second lesson. Ask the groups to consider any changes in their views. Ask them to come up with reasons for any changes that might have occurred in their ratings.

Finally, ask these same groups to discuss the character to whom they found it easiest to relate. Ask the students to share why this was the case with the other members of their group.

In some programmes, teachers will link the outcomes and activities in the one section of the programme. The following example from a grade 1 class illustrates this approach. It is the writing section of the programme. Once again, it utilizes the outcomes that are provided as part of the NSW English syllabus. Teachers from other countries can use a similar approach utilizing their own syllabus or curriculum outcomes or attainments.

Sample programme segment for writing
Class: grade 1
Duration: two weeks
Programme content:

This programme segment would follow an outline of a number of generic writing components which would describe the procedures to be followed in regular 'writing workshops', the use of writing conferences, and the general approach used to foster student spelling. In essence, the class would have a writing workshop of 30–45 minutes' duration four times per week in which they would write, have conferences and be given mini-lessons on writing. The following are focused writing lessons planned to target specific outcomes.

Week 1

Lesson 1

Related outcome (from the syllabus):

Writes brief imaginative and factual texts which include some related ideas about familiar topics.

English learning experiences:

As part of science have students record observations concerning one of the following:

- behaviour of the class rabbit during a period of observation;
- amount of litter that is found on the classroom floor at the end of the day;
- weather changes each hour during the school day.

Prior to this activity demonstrate how one records observations of this type. Jointly construct a set of observations using the whole class as participants utilizing a different example to the above.

Lesson 2

Related outcome (from the syllabus):

Uses wordprocessing programmes to create texts.

English learning experiences:

In pairs give the students the opportunity to turn their observations from the previous lesson into a recount of the experience. Once again, demonstrate the writing of a recount and jointly construct a text using the material generated in the previous lesson when demonstrating how to make observational notes.

WEEK 2

Lesson 1

Related outcome (from the syllabus):

Writes brief imaginative and factual texts which include some related ideas about familiar topics.

English learning experiences:

Have the students use written conversation with a friend. Start by demonstrating this form of writing using the board or an overhead projector and involving a number of students in the class in this joint construction.

Note: Written conversation (as its name implies) involves students engaging in a form of written dialogue with another student. The conversation begins with a statement about themselves or some common item of interest. The first statement often ends with a question (but doesn't have to). The person's partner then responds in writing. The conversation continues for a set period of time (not more than 15 minutes for students of this age) or until students run out of things to say (Figure 8.1).

Lesson 2

Related outcome (from the syllabus):

Uses some basic linguistic structures and features of written language so that writing can be readily interpreted by others.

English learning experiences:

Introduce the use of personal letters as a form of writing. Show and read examples of personal letters and discuss the linguistic features of each. Using an example show the students that letters usually begin with an outline of past experiences (since the person last wrote) in chronological order, and then this is followed by personal comments and occasionally questions or specific greetings.

Jointly construct a letter as a class using someone known to all (e.g. another teacher) therefore allowing an authentic audience and the chance of a written response.

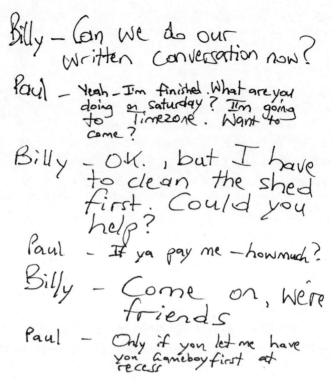

Figure 8.1 An example of a written conversation

Provide an opportunity for students to write a letter to another person. This might be a family member or perhaps a penfriend from another class which you have arranged.

DETAILS ON ASSESSMENT

Another important part of any programme is a section on assessment. As outlined in Chapter 7, assessment should always be seen as integral to the teaching and learning process. As such, it will normally relate closely to the content of the programme and the expected outcomes. Some teachers prefer simply to write an assessment and evaluation section at the end of each lesson outlined or programme segment. Such statements make explicit how the teacher will judge whether learning has taken place. The following comments are typical:

Assess the extent to which students understood the basic linguistic components of letter writing and were able to complete a letter to a friend. Did the student manage to use accurate punctuation and spelling? Was the meaning of the letter clear? Was the letter interesting and engaging for the reader?

Assess the extent to which all students were able to make observations. Did they follow the task? How detailed were their written observations? Were the observations varied and seemingly accurate? Were the notes written able to be followed by the student and his/her partner?

Another approach to assessment is to include a much broader statement at the end of a programme segment. In this case the assessment is still integral to teaching and learning, but the programme entry is more general in nature. For example:

Assessment in this four-week programme on *The Pinballs* will include: consideration of student engagement in the tasks; the extent to which the students are able to identify evidence of the author's views on stereotypes; understanding of the major themes examined; depth of analysis of characterization; quality of responses to specific lessons.

In this four-week writing programme the focus of my assessment will link closely with the major stated expected outcomes. The key questions that will be used to address this are: Did the students show control over the specific text form that was required? Did the students show appropriate attention to spelling, grammar and punctuation (this is related of course to the purpose of the writing)? Did the students' writing gain the interest of readers?

RESOURCES

The final component of most teachers' programmes is the resource section. For some teachers this is simply a list of resource materials located in the classroom. For others it may well incorporate segments from commercial resources which act as part of the programme, or it could be a set of blackline masters, examples of worksheets, lists of children's literature to be read, potential writing topics, detailed notes on specific aspects of the programmes (e.g. notes on specific written genres) and so on. Once again, the manner in which teachers present this section varies greatly.

Conclusion

Programming is a highly individual process. The above is designed simply to act as a guide to possibilities. There are obviously many other possibilities. In some countries the programme is redundant because what is taught matches closely to the syllabus or curriculum. Teachers who face such an educational system may supplement the given syllabus with a day book which usually contains procedural information concerning the resources to be used, the timing of activities and so on.

Other variations occur in schools where teachers team teach, necessitating programmes which are jointly constructed with someone else. This may mean that the teacher only writes half of the programme. In some school systems specialist teachers are used for subjects like science and technology, and hence some aspects of the literacy programme are developed by another teacher. Hence, great diversity can occur in various constraints that can invariably have an effect on the teacher's programme.

Irrespective of the form and process used to develop programmes it is important for the principles outlined at the start of this chapter to be observed, and for programming to contribute to the quality of the teaching and learning that occurs in your classroom. It must not simply be a requirement imposed by someone else. Programming is important and, when done well, will lead to more effective teaching.

Having reached the point in this book of discussing programming and assessment one could be forgiven for thinking that nothing else remains to be said. However, all that I have said in the previous chapters suggests that my approach to education is one of openness and constant preparedness to consider change to the way students are taught, and multiple pathways to literacy. Consistent with this total philosophy is my desire to consider several key issues that are currently a source of puzzlement and reflection. These issues will be discussed in Chapter 9.

CHAPTER 9
Tackling the tough questions

While this book has addressed a range of issues concerned with literacy and has attempted to outline basic principles and procedures to ensure that literacy is attainable for all, I would not want to end by suggesting that meeting people's literacy needs is a simple process. It isn't! Literacy, as has been argued throughout this book, is a complex cultural practice. Written literacy is but one of many sign systems (others include drawing, speaking, acting, various broadcast media, Braille codes, etc.), each of which offers humans the potential to make sense of their world and to share their understandings with others. Literacy is a set of cultural practices which has the potential to permit or deny access to a range of other cultural practices and institutions, including education, employment, membership of specific social groups and roles. As a consequence, literacy is not seen by all as the panacea for all social problems. Indeed, many postmodern critics see it as 'toxic', and 'discriminating'; an almost 'viral' practice that perpetuates social inequalities. Graff (1987) has even suggested that the traditionally accepted wisdom that literacy leads to achievement, higher-order thinking ability, social growth and personal empowerment, is a myth.

Apple argues (in Willinsky, 1990) that societies reproduce themselves in and through the rhythms and textures of culture, consciousness and everyday life. The relations of inequality that dominate our society are reproduced, and contested, in the mundane activities that organize life. Daily activities like literacy can act as forms of regulation and exploitation, as well as potential modes of resistance and solidarity. Literacy can act to produce a shared system of beliefs and values and to create national and ideological unity (see also Batsleer *et al.*, 1985; Luke, 1988).

However, while recognizing that literacy has the potential to disempower as well as empower, I still believe that it is an important cultural practice to which everyone should have access. The ability to use literacy for self-defined purposes is a basic human right.

Hence all teachers have a responsibility to contribute to the correcting of the injustices that occur in relation to access to literacy. The starting point for doing this is for us to recognize some of the injustices of school literacy which are invariably mirrored (some would also argue for the reverse) in society. Edelsky (1991) suggests that this involves recognizing that 'the texts, voices and interests of the dominant drown out those of the subordinate' (p. 2). However, Edelsky reminds us that while educational practices can reproduce social hierarchies, schools can also be the sites for challenging these hierarchies. As a result she advocates 'transformative educational practices' as the appropriate response of teachers and schools to their observation of injustice. This clearly echoes the position of this book, which right from its first chapter has stressed the need to do more than critique the practice of schooling. Rather, we need to transform schooling and the place that literacy has in it. The title of this book is reflective of this desire and makes it clear that there are multiple pathways to literacy, which will invariably reflect the characteristics of literacy learners, teachers, schools and communities. The pathways metaphor is also related to the belief that literacy will take each literacy user somewhere. It will provide access to learning, educational possibilities, life pursuits and culture.

The challenge that faces us as teachers is enormous, because we seek to undertake this transformative work within contexts, in communities, and with people who have already made up their minds about what literacy is and how it should be used. We need to challenge ourselves and others to consider the essential nature of literacy and return to the questions I posed in Chapter 1: Why is it that school literacy disempowers some, and empowers others? How must schools change in order to ensure that literacy is empowering for all? What types of classroom environments permit all children to gain access to the literacy practices which they need to take their place in the world? How must schools change in order to ensure that literacy is empowering for all?

As I also pointed out in Chapter 1, schools are among the most stable institutions in society, and are in need of reform. Social evolutionary development is imperative; we need to provide alternative opportunities and practices which challenge existing educational practices. The previous eight chapters have attempted to provide an insight into how this might occur. I have attempted to show how classrooms can be changed and how programmes can be responsive to the diverse cultures and needs of our students, so that the multiple pathways of which I speak can be opened up. But if we are to continue to open up pathways for our students we need to continue to tussle with some of the difficult issues that confront us. As a consequence, I want to end this book by challenging readers to reconsider the place that schools hold in society and the relationship that they have with their wider communities. Let me leave you with three challenges.

A challenge to seek justice

I have spoken much about the role that literacy has both to empower and disempower. We need to do more than simply talk about this. For example, as an Australian I need to ask myself: why is it that Aboriginal and Torres Strait Islander Australians still struggle to succeed in our education system? Why do they leave school earlier? Why do they have higher levels of unemployment? Why do they have higher infant mortality rates and higher levels of specific diseases? What role does education play in addressing some of these issues, or perhaps even acting to inadvertently sustain such inequalities? Furthermore, how is literacy implicated in all of this?

But looking more globally, while there are countries and regions in our world where the majority of children still do not go to school (e.g. sub-Saharan Africa), in 'developed' countries many young people are fleeing our schools because they do not see them as relevant to their lives. How can we address the needs of 30 per cent of the world's population who still cannot read and write? How do we respond to the reality that two-thirds of these people are women? It is interesting to note that the so-called literacy problems of the 'developed' world are quite different from those of the 'underdeveloped' world. In the former, there is almost universal literacy, but some would claim there are 10 to 30 per cent of the populations of countries like England, Australia and the United States who struggle to use literacy for the varied purposes necessary in their daily lives. Literacy for these people is a problem because of its impact on their ability to cope in a print-rich world and their access to education, training and employment. In the case of the latter, some countries have levels of illiteracy of 70 per cent, and hence literacy is vital for improvements in community health, development of agricultural practices that will address food shortages, and the fight against specific diseases.

In the 'developed' countries access to literacy is more of a problem for boys and men, whereas in the 'underdeveloped' countries it is far more of a problem for girls and women (Cairney, 1994a). However, the world is never as simple as this, for in both 'developed' and 'underdeveloped' countries there are many inequities that are invisible. One example, of course, is the dominance of male characters and stereotypes in texts of almost every type including literature, newspapers and the broadcast media. In 'developed' countries there are many writers who would argue that one of the greatest inequalities of literacy is the portrayal of women in literature (see Gilbert, 1989; Luke and Luke, 1989; Gilbert and Taylor, 1991; Davies, 1993 for a full discussion). The development of 'readers who read' (the focus of Chapter 5) obviously involves developing readers who can 'read against the grain', who 'resist' the stereotypes and ideologies that writers can knowingly and unknowingly direct at the reader.

How do we respond to these issues? How can our school systems be more responsive to the needs of all students and their families. One of the great challenges for all teachers is to cope with a changed world and to be responsive to its needs. At the same time, the school does have a role as a preserver of culture. The problem is, which culture(s)? We need to constantly ask ourselves: whose culture do my school, my classroom, and my practices privilege? And whose culture do they ignore, and perhaps even devalue?

A challenge to rethink the forms of and possibilities for literacy

There is no doubt that we live in an age where literacy is probably more pervasive than ever before. But while this is so, we are surrounded by numerous literacy anomalies. More books are written, libraries hold more books, and more books are purchased than ever before in the history of humankind. And yet, reading as a leisure pursuit, or for self-directed learning, appears to be in decline.

Literacy is now expected to be used in almost every occupation in 'developed' countries, and yet in some countries (e.g. the USA) questions have been raised in government reports about the ability of schools to develop readers and writers who can use literacy in the workplace. Literacy and schooling have never been so highly valued, and yet teachers have never been valued so little in many countries and cultures.

Schools are among the most stable and unchanging institutions, and yet it is obvious that change is needed in the 1990s. True, teachers are constantly seeking new professional insights and ideas, and new curriculum materials are always being sought, but change is often slow. One area where this is apparent is in the very texts we use and the way they are encountered.

We live in an age where written text bombards our environment. Children living in the post-Spielberg age encounter numerous texts daily. But outside school most are short, and are delivered via billboards, magazines, television, computer games, videos, clothing and so on. Books are rarely the source of the texts that bombard us outside school. And yet, written texts presented in a variety of paper forms (particularly books) dominate our schools.

This presents schools with a problem. Do we accept this and reduce school to a mere reflection of a world where the '30 second grab' is seemingly the limit to one's concentration or commitment to anything? My answer is no! However, if we do not start to recognize the enormous differences between the traditional literacy of schooling and that of the wider world, schools and teachers will increasingly be seen as of little relevance and value.

I have no doubt that books will continue to have a place in our world, but increasingly visual and written texts will be delivered electronically. Some of us can remember a time before television, but none of the students we teach in 'developed' countries can (and the same is true of fax machines, videos, satellite broadcasts, etc.). The influence of television has been significant, but schools have still not harnessed its potential. While in most countries we can see evidence of programmes for children and schools being developed, the potential is still largely untapped. In a recent study of the literacy practices of students in the transition years of schooling from primary to high school (see Cairney *et al.*, 1995), virtually no use of television was observed in classrooms. And yet television, like books, has the potential to introduce students to 'worlds' that are well beyond their experiences in forms that many find easier to access. There is also great potential to bring written literacy and television together as powerful allies. Foreign language teachers have already recognized the potential that subtitles in television programmes have as a vehicle for language learning. In Australia, more recently, an adult literacy programme has been developed for television called the *Reading and Writing Roadshow*. Clearly, the potential is great.

There is little doubt that the next decade will see the dramatically increased use of computers and a range of interactive technologies that will couple computers (e.g. television, radio, telephones). Already, virtually everyone in 'developed' countries has almost daily contact with computers and computer literacy. And yet, schools have been relatively untouched by computers and other related technology. In the same study in which little television use was detected (Cairney *et al.*, 1995) computers were almost invisible. While one could point to exciting and innovative school practices in Australia and many other countries, this is not the case in most schools. In Australia, for example, the average primary classroom (if it is lucky) will have a single computer (probably obsolete compared to those in the market-place and the home) and a limited range of software, most of which consists of games or basic drill material for mathematics and spelling or vocabulary. Children in such classes have probably used the computer a number of times during the year, but it is unlikely that many students use it regularly for wordprocessing, accessing databases and communicating with other students electronically.

There is enormous untapped potential in the technology that is dominating the world of business, retail industry, telecommunications and universities. Schools need to respond to this and use it. The following are examples of the exciting opportunities that could exist for our children right now.

- Electronic mail communication with students in other countries to learn about their culture.
- Delivery of film, video, and live programmes from around the world on any topic.
- Access to thousands of databases around the world containing information on limitless topics.
- Electronic access to encyclopaedias, dictionaries, atlases, thesauruses, etc., with instant search and retrieval functions.
- Presentation via computer (using CD ROM) of interactive texts that utilize words, visual images, sound and moving pictures.
- Access to electronically delivered books, magazines and newspapers.

- Electronic access to primary historical source material normally archived in the world's great libraries and museums.
- Membership of 'listservers' which are essentially 'bulletin boards' for communities of people who communicate with each other about topics of mutual interest (this electronic mail function is currently used widely in universities).
- The power to store, manipulate, and even interpret large amounts of information.

These are just some of the almost limitless uses of technology; and literacy is involved in every function. While the traditional book and the use of pen and paper will still have a place (for a time?), it seems almost inevitable that one day most use of literacy will be via electronic means. Doubters suggest that the book will never be replaced because of its convenience and aesthetic qualities. We've all heard people say 'You can't curl up with a computer'. Well, the reality is that you can; the pocket electronic book has been with us for a number of years and will soon be widely available. Many parents will testify that computer games already find their way under the bed covers (some with purpose-built illuminated screens). Schools must make a quantum leap in this area to avoid yet another reason for our communities to see us as irrelevant.

A challenge to develop partnerships with our communities

Schools in the 1990s have an unusual relationship with their communities. All teachers see that schools must have a relationship to their communities and in particular to the parents of their students, but frequently this does not go beyond a range of 'tokenistic' opportunities for parents to have access to information about schooling. Parent and community involvement is obviously very important (Epstein, 1983; Delgado-Gaitan, 1991). We know, for example, that there is a high positive correlation between parent knowledge, beliefs and interactive styles and children's school achievement (see Schaefer, 1991 for a detailed review). We also know that differences in family backgrounds appear to account for a large share of variance in student achievement. School factors (e.g. resources, class sizes, classroom organization and methods) simply cannot account for the variability that occurs in student achievement (Jencks *et al.*, 1972; Hanusheck, 1981; Thompson, 1985). It is apparent that social influences outside the school also contribute to the variations in student achievement. Some have gone so far as to suggest that the cumulative effect of a range of home-related factors probably accounts for the greatest proportion of variability in student achievement (Rutter *et al.*, 1970; Thompson, 1985).

Attempts to explain this relationship have varied, but it is obvious that a number reflect deficit models, and are based on the assumption that some children receive 'good' or 'appropriate' preparation for schooling, while others receive 'poor' or 'inappropriate' preparation. This view has been criticized because of its failure to recognize that schooling is a cultural practice (Auerbach, 1989). What it ignores is the fact that much of the variability of student achievement in school reflects discrepancies that exist between school resources and instructional methods, and the cultural practices of the home (Heath, 1983; Au and Kawakami, 1984; Cazden, 1988; Moll, 1988).

As I have argued in Chapter 1, we know that schools engage in specific discourses and hence inconsistently tap the social and cultural resources of society, privileging specific groups by emphasizing particular linguistic styles, curricula and authority patterns (Bourdieu, 1977). As Gee (1990) has claimed, to be a teacher in any school demands specific ways of using language, behaving, interacting, and adhering to sets of values and attitudes. There is obvious potential for mismatches between these discourses and those which have been characteristic of some children's homes and communities.

What matters is not literacy as an isolated skill, but the social practices into which people are enculturated (or apprenticed) as members of a specific social group (Scribner and Cole, 1981). Not surprisingly, one gets better at specific social practices as one practises them. It would seem that those children who enter school already having been partially apprenticed into the social practices of schooling (of which literacy is a part) invariably perform better at the practices of schooling right from the start.

As I have argued in Chapter 1, and elsewhere (Cairney, 1994b; Cairney and Munsie, 1992b), the most effective response to this situation is not to keep telling schools that they need to change (this does little other than further privileging the 'tellers'), but rather to engage in social evolutionary development by providing opportunities and alternative practices which challenge existing educational practices and facilitate new and genuine partnerships between schools and communities.

Involving parents more closely in school education has the potential to develop new understanding by each party of the other's specific cultural practices. This, in turn, may well enable both teachers and parents to understand the way each defines, values and uses literacy as part of cultural practices (Cairney, 1994b, 1995). In this way schooling can be adjusted to meet the needs of families. Parents in turn can also be given the opportunity to observe and understand the definitions of literacy that schools support, and which ultimately empower individuals to take their place in society. Teachers have a significant responsibility to accept change. Gee (1990, p. 67) suggests that English teachers need to accept their role as socializers, and reflect critically, comparatively and with a 'sense of the possibilities for change'.

However, our early attempts to involve families more fully in their children's literacy learning have taken many forms, and at times have been anything but helpful. Briggs and Potter (1990) point out that parent involvement programmes are often shallow, ineffectual, confusing, and frustrating to both parents and teachers. As a result, evidence of significant outcomes is difficult to find in the literature.

As I have outlined elsewhere (e.g. Cairney, 1994b, 1995), notable recent programmes have included Project FLAME (Shanahan and Rodriguez-Brown, 1993), the initiatives of the Illinois Literacy Resource Development Center (ILRDC, 1990), and Schools Reaching Out (Jackson et al., 1994). Unlike many of the early parent literacy programmes, these programmes have attempted to develop a sense of partnership with parents and communities. As such, they have attempted to recognize the significant cultural differences between communities, and to adapt programmes accordingly. These programmes have recognized that relationships between home and school achievement are complex, and as a result require initiatives that do more than simply offer parents information.

In Australia, there have also been a number of significant initiatives in Family Literacy. However, most have as yet not really led to the development of real partnerships between schools and communities. Nevertheless, these programmes have had an impact. Several have been designed so that the resulting materials can be used easily in a variety of locations. These programmes are typically designed for schools to use according to their purposes. One such programme developed by Sue Hill for parents of younger children is Read with Me (DEET, 1992). It was developed in a disadvantaged school and consists of two workshops built around a video and an attractively presented parent book. It is designed for parents with children aged 4 to 8 years, and aims to share ideas on the ways parents read with their children.

Other examples are focused on the needs of children who have experienced literacy difficulties. One of the best-known examples of this type is the Parent Tutors Program, which was developed by Max Kemp (1989). The programme is made up of ten seminars designed to give parents an understanding of how learning is affected by different conditions and methods of teaching. The seminar's emphasis is on assisting parents to give skilled help in the home in reading and writing, spelling, information gathering and time organization. It is designed for children aged 7 to 15 years who have been referred to the Centre for special help with literacy.

Other programmes have been focused on specific parent target groups. For example, the Parents as Tutors programme (Ministry of Education and Training, Victoria) was developed for children and parents in disadvantaged schools as a joint initiative of the Inner City Support Centre, DSP and the Brash Foundation. It aims to assist parents to support their children and is designed for parents with children in the pre-school and primary years.

Two programmes that I have been involved with closely are the Talk to a Literacy Learner (TTALL) and Effective Partners in Secondary Literacy Learning (EPISLL) programmes (Cairney and Munsie, 1993a, 1993b, 1995; Cairney, 1995). These quite ambitious programmes were designed to focus on parents, but with the aim of involving teachers, students and their parents in a partnership that would help students cope more effectively with the literacy demands of schooling. The TTALL programme was designed to involve parents more closely in the literacy development of their pre-school and primary school children. It attempts to achieve this through an eight-week series of sixteen two-hour interactive workshops, each of which is integrated with observation of literacy learners, classroom visits, practice of strategies, and a variety of home-tasks.

The EPISLL programme was an outgrowth of the TTALL programme (Cairney and Munsie, 1992c) and is designed for parents of secondary aged children. It consists of eleven two-hour sessions that cover topics as diverse as reading and writing across the curriculum, learning, study, coping with teenagers, research work, and using resources. This programme was developed at the request of parents who had been part of the TTALL programme but who wanted more help with the support of their secondary school children. Parents were involved at every stage of the development and implementation of this project. Like the TTALL project it has led to a programme which is now being used in many schools. Both programmes have been evaluated and have been shown to have positive outcomes for parents, students, teachers and schools (Cairney and Munsie, 1992b, 1993a, 1995; Cairney, 1995).

The brief description of some of the programmes that have been offered should give some sense of the variety of initiatives that have taken place. However, there is a sameness about many of the programmes that have been devised and many do not move far towards partnership with parents and communities. Typically, they are initiated by schools, researchers or educational curriculum experts and have been based very much within the school. Most have led to the development of a package or programme which can then be replicated at other sites. However, as I have pointed out elsewhere (Cairney and Munsie, 1992a), Family Literacy initiatives can (and should) take many forms.

In attempting to move towards closer partnership with parents and communities I have suggested (Cairney, 1991; Cairney and Munsie, 1992b) that we should address four variables when assessing the worth and effectiveness of such programmes:

Content – What information is shared? What is the focus of group discussions, demonstrations, home-tasks and so on? What is the stated purpose of the content?

Process – How is information shared? Who acts as the facilitator or leader for any programme and how does this person structure opportunities for discussion, observation, etc?

Source – Who has initiated the involvement? Was it a parent, school, community, or government initiative?

Control – Who is in control of the programme? Where is the programme located (home, school, community building)? How do

189

parents become involved in programmes (chosen, selected, parent initiative)? Does it address parent and community needs?

When assessing the worth of any initiative, consideration of criteria like the above is important. For example, while many programmes claim to 'involve' parents, or attempt to develop 'partnerships', one needs to test these claims. Can any programme lead to partnership if the initiator of the programme is the school, with no attempt to involve parents in its planning and conduct. Some have begun to question the programmes that have been implemented. For example, Auerbach (1989) has argued that some programmes are based simply on models designed to transmit school practices to the home. Criticism has also been directed at those programmes that are designed to exert a central influence on parents' caregiving roles (often referred to as 'intergenerational' literacy programmes). The aim of some of these programmes is to 'improve' the education of caregivers in order to bring about changes in children's learning. However, as Cairney and Munsie (1992b) have pointed out, such aims are based on a number of myths, including the belief that some parents are 'better' parents than others. Such judgements are culturally laden and need to be challenged. Thinking of this type is based on very narrow definitions of parent involvement, and leads to schools seeking to determine what parents can do for teachers, or how schools can make parents 'better' at their role in the home. Instead, what we need to address is how schools and parents can develop close relationships of mutual support and trust, which will ultimately lead to schools that are seen as more adequately addressing family and community needs.

What schools need to consider is not how more knowledge can be transmitted from schools to parents and their children, but rather, how schools and communities can move towards mutual consensus about schooling. This process of reaching shared understanding is what Vygotsky called 'intersubjectivity' (1978), and describes a process of reaching a shared focus of attention and mutual understanding of any joint activity.

It is important to stress that what I am arguing for here is a two-sided process which involves providing parents and communities with access to the practices of schooling (and how these are supported) but at the same time opening up the community to the school so that a greater recognition of its values, expectations and literacy practices can have an impact on the shaping of schooling. As I have argued in Chapters 1 and 2, there are mismatches between home and school literacy practices, which inevitably make it more difficult for some students to succeed at school.

Involving parents more closely in school education has the potential to develop new understanding by each party of the other's specific cultural practices and lead to the type of 'reciprocity' which Harry (1992) argues is needed. Teachers and parents do need to understand the way each defines, values and uses literacy as part of cultural practices. Such mutual understanding offers the potential for schooling to be adjusted to meet the needs of families. In addition, it offers parents the opportunity to observe and understand the literacy of schooling, a literacy which ultimately empowers individuals to take their place in society (Cairney, 1994b, 1995).

Where do we go to from here?

I wanted to finish this book with my challenge to develop partnerships with our communities because I believe that this is the single most important issue of the 1990s. We know that there are many challenges for teachers. Being a teacher in the 1990s is harder than ever before. As people expect more of education and literacy, obviously more will be expected of those who are the 'keepers' of both. Schools are still struggling to change and reform themselves in ways consistent with a changed world. This requires us to be more responsive to our communities and to be more reflective of their diversity. In an age of instant communication it is impossible to ignore such human diversity. And yet, far too often schools appear to be failing to recognize and address this diversity. There are multiple pathways to literacy, reflecting the multiple literacies and diverse communities that schools serve. While there is always a tension between reflecting culture and shaping it (for this is a reciprocal relationship), schools must address the problem of clinging to practices that effectively perpetuate the inequities that we see across our world and also (in microcosm) in our classes.

I have been asking myself a number of questions of late about my own practices and those of schooling more generally (see also Cairney, 1994b, 1995):

Do the literacy practices of my classroom disempower some, and empower others?

If so, which students are disadvantaged most by the types of literacy practices I support and legitimize?

How representative are the literacy practices of my classroom of the diversity of literacy practices that students will encounter outside school?

How must I change my practices in order to ensure that literacy can meet the diverse literacy backgrounds and needs of my students?

How can I set up classroom and school environments that permit intersubjectivity to develop between students, parents, and teachers?

Gee (1990, p. 67) has suggested that 'short of radical social change' there is 'no access to power in society without control over the social practices in thought, speech and writing essay-text literacy and its attendant world view'. We need to ask constantly, what does this mean for the way literacy is defined and used in classrooms?

As teachers I am sure we are committed to seeing all students acquire the literacy practices that are necessary for them to take on the roles they define for themselves in an increasingly more complex world. In addition, I am equally certain that all teachers are concerned for those around the world who do not have access to literacy; not to mention those who can read and write, but find it difficult to use relevant literacy practices for a range of social purposes. Arguing over 'better' methodology is not the solution. Instead, we need to engage in social evolutionary development by providing opportunities and alternative programmes and curricula which challenge existing educational practices and open up the multiple pathways that I have spoken of often throughout this book. These pathways must be as diverse as the students and their needs. We live in exciting and yet challenging times. I am confident that schools can adapt to our more complex world and seek equitable practices and outcomes for all students. I encourage you the reader actively to seek to open up pathways to literacy for all students.

References

Ahlberg, J. and Ahlberg, A. (1986) *The Jolly Postman: Or Other People's Letters*. London: Heinemann.

Anderson, R. C. and Biddle, W. B. (1975) On asking people questions about what they are reading. In G. H. Bower (ed.), *The Psychology of Learning and Motivation*, vol. 9. London: Academic Press.

Anstey, M. and Bull, G. (1989) From teaching to learning: translating monitoring into planning and practice. In E. Daly (ed.), *Monitoring Children's Language Development*. Melbourne: Australian Reading Association, pp. 3–15.

Atwell, N. (1987) *In the Middle: Writing, Reading and Learning with Adolescents*. Portsmouth, NH: Heinemann.

Au, K. and Kawakami, A. (1984) Vygotskian perspectives on discussion processes in small-group reading lessons. In P. Peterson and L. C. Wilkinson (eds), *The Social Context of Instruction*. Portsmouth, NH: Heinemann, pp. 209–25.

Auerbach, E. (1989) Toward a social-contextual approach to family literacy. *Harvard Educational Review* **59**, 165–81.

Baker, C. D. and Freebody, P. (1989) *Children's First Schoolbooks: Introductions to the Culture of Literacy*. Oxford: Blackwell.

Bakhtin, M. (1929/1973) *Problems of Dostoevsky's Poetics* (trans. R. W. Rotsel, 1973). Ann Arbor, MI: Ardis.

Bakhtin, M. (1935/1981) Discourse in the novel. In M. Holquist (ed.), *The Dialogic Imagination*. Austin, TX: University of Texas Press. (Original work published 1935.)

Balota, D., Pollatsek, A. and Rayner, K. (1985) The interaction of contextual constraints and parafoveal visual information in reading. *Cognitive Psychology* **17**, 364–90.

Barnes, D. (1976) *From Communication to Curriculum*. London: Penguin.

Barnes, D., Britton, J. and Rosen, H. (1971) *Language, the Learner and the School*. Harmondsworth, Middlesex, UK: Penguin.

Barrett, T. (1976) Taxonomy of reading comprehension. In R. Smith and T. C. Barrett, *Teaching Reading in the Middle Grades*. Reading, MA: Addison-Wesley.

Barthes, R. (1979) From work to text. In J. V. Harari (ed.), *Textual Strategies: Perspectives in Post-Structural Criticism*. Ithaca, NY: Cornell University Press.

Bates, D. (1989) *The New Writer's Survival Guide*. Ringwood, Vic.: Penguin.

Batsleer, J., Davies, T., O'Rourke, R. and Weedon, C. (1985) *Rewriting English*. New York: Methuen.

Bawden, N. A. (1967) *Handful of Thieves*. London: Lippincott.

Beck, I. L., McKeown, M. G., McCaslin, E. S. and Burkes, A. M. (1979) *Instructional Dimensions That May Affect Reading Comprehension: Examples from Two Commercial Reading Programs*. Pittsburgh: University of Pittsburgh, Learning Research Development Center.

Bernstein, B. (1971) *Class, Codes and Control: Theoretical Studies towards a Sociology of Language*, vol. 1. London: Routledge & Kegan Paul.

Bernstein, B. (1973) *Class, Codes and Control: Applied Studies towards a Sociology of Language*, vol. 2. London: Routledge & Kegan Paul.

Bleich, D. (1978) *Subjective Criticism*. Baltimore: Johns Hopkins University Press.

Bloom, B. S. (1956) *Taxonomy of Educational Objectives, Handbook I: Cognitive Domain*. New York: David McKay.

Bloome, D. (1985a) Reading as a social process. *Language Arts* **62**(2).

Bloome, D. (ed.) (1985b) *Classrooms and Literacy*. Norwood, NJ: Ablex.

Bloome, D. (ed.) (1987) *Literacy and Schooling*. Norwood, NJ: Ablex.

Bloome, D. and Egan-Robertson, A. (1993) The social construction of inter-textuality in classroom reading and writing lessons. *Reading Research Quarterly* **28**(4), 305–33.

Blyton, Enid (1937) *Adventures of the Wishing Chair*. London: Newnes.

Blyton, E. (1939) *The Enchanted Wood*. London: Darrel Waters.

Blyton, E. (1943) *The Magic Faraway Tree*. London: Darrel Waters.

Bourdieu, P. (1977) Cultural reproduction and social reproduction. In J. Karabel and A. H. Halsey (eds), *Power and Ideology in Education*. New York: Oxford University Press.

Briggs, F. and Potter, G. (1990) *Teaching Children in the First Three Years of School*. Melbourne: Longman Cheshire.

Britton, J. (1970) *Language and Learning*. London: Allen Lane.

Britton, J., Burgess, T., Martin, N., McLeod, A. and Rosen, H. (1975) *The Development of Writing Abilities (11–18)*. London: Macmillan.

Bruner, J. (1983) *Child's Talk: Learning To Use Language*. Oxford: Oxford University Press.

Bruner, J. (1986) *Actual Minds, Possible Worlds*. Cambridge, MA: Harvard University Press.

Byars, B. (1977) *The Pinballs*. London: Bodley Head.

Cairney, T. H. (1981) There's more to editing than meets the eye. *Reading Around* **9** (4).

Cairney, T. H. (1982) When I was a parking meter. *Primary Journal* **1**.

Cairney, T. H. (1983/1990) *Balancing the Basics*, 2nd edn. Gosford, NSW: Ashton Scholastic.

Cairney, T. H. (1985) Linking reading and writing. In D. Burnes, H. French and F. Moore (eds), *Literacy: Strategies and Perspectives*. Adelaide: Australian Reading Association, pp. 11–18.

Cairney, T. H. (1986) *Helping Children To Make Meaning – Ten Literature-based Activities for Developing Literacy*. Wagga Wagga: Riverina Literacy Centre Publications.

Cairney, T. H. (1987a) The social foundations of literacy. *Australian Journal of Reading* **10** (2).

Cairney, T. H. (1987b) Supporting the independent learner: negotiating change in the classroom. In J. Hancock and B. Comber (eds), *Independent Learners at School*. Sydney: Methuen.

Cairney, T. H. (1988a) The influence of intertextuality upon the reading and writing of children aged 6–12 years. Paper presented to the World Reading Congress, Gold Coast, Australia.

Cairney, T. H. (ed.) (1988b) *Pieces of Our World*. Wagga Wagga: Wagga Education Centre.

Cairney, T. H. (1989) Text talk: helping students to learn about language. *English in Australia* **90**.

Cairney, T. H. (1990a) *Other Worlds: The Endless Possibilities of Literature*. Portsmouth, NH: Heinemann.

Cairney, T. H. (1990b) *Teaching Reading Comprehension: Meaning Makers at Work*. Milton Keynes: Open University Press.

Cairney, T. H. (1990c). Intertextuality: Infectious echoes from the past. *The Reading Teacher* **43** (7), 478–85.

Cairney, T. H. (1991) Talking to literacy learners: the impact of an education programme upon parent/child interactions. Paper presented to the International Convention on Language and Learning, Norwich, 6–10 April.

Cairney, T. H. (1992a) Stirring the cauldron: fostering the development of students' intertextual histories. *Language Arts* **69** (6).

Cairney, T. H. (1992b). Mountain or mole hill: the genre debate viewed from 'Down Under'. *Reading* (UK) **26** (2).

Cairney, T. H. (1994a) *Report of the UNESCO World Symposium on Family Literacy*, Paris, 3–5 October.

Cairney, T. H. (1994b) Family literacy: moving towards new partnerships in education. *Australian Journal of Language and Literacy* **17** (4), 262–75.

Cairney, T. H. (1995) Developing parent partnerships in secondary literacy learning. *Journal of Reading* **48** (5).

Cairney, T. H. and Langbien, S. (1989) Building communities of readers and writers. *The Reading Teacher* **42** (8), 560–7.

Cairney, T. H., Lowe, K., McKenzie, P. and Petrakis, D. (1993) *Literacy and Youth: Extending Literacy Success Beyond Institutional Care.* Final report of DEET funded project. Sydney: UWS Nepean Press.

Cairney, T. H., Lowe, K. and Sproats, E. (1995) *Literacy in Transition: An Investigation of Literacy Practices Across the Primary-Secondary Divide.* Final report to the Department of Employment Education and Training. Sydney: DEET.

Cairney, T. H. and Munsie, L. (1992a) Talking to Literacy Learners: a parent education project. *Reading* (UK) **26** (4).

Cairney, T. H. and Munsie, L. (1992b) *Beyond Tokenism: Parents as Partners in Literacy Learning.* Melbourne: Australian Reading Association.

Cairney, T. H. and Munsie, L. (1992c) *Talk to a Literacy Learner.* Sydney: UWS Press.

Cairney, T. H. and Munsie, L. (1993a) *Effective Partners in Secondary Literacy Learning: Final Report to the Disadvantaged Schools Program.* Sydney: UWS Press.

Cairney, T. H. and Munsie, L. (1993b) *Effective Partners in Secondary Literacy Learning Program.* Sydney: UWS Press.

Cairney, T. H. and Munsie, L. (1995) Parent participation in literacy learning. *The Reading Teacher* **48** (5).

Calkins, L. M. (1986) *The Art of Teaching Writing.* Portsmouth, NH: Heinemann.

Calkins, L. M. (1991) *Living Between the Lines.* Portsmouth, NH: Heinemann.

Cambourne, B. (1988) *The Whole Story: Natural Learning and the Acquisition of Literacy in the Classroom.* Sydney: Ashton Scholastic.

Cambourne, B. and Turbill, J. (1990) Assessment in whole language classrooms: theory into practice. *Elementary School Journal* **90** (3), 337–49.

Carle, E. (1969) *The Very Hungry Caterpillar.* London: Hamish Hamilton.

Carner, R. L. (1963) Levels of questioning. *Education* **83**.

Cazden, C. (1988) *Classroom Discourse: The Language of Teaching and Learning.* Portsmouth, NH: Heinemann.

Chomsky, C. (1970) Reading, writing and phonology. *Harvard Educational Review* **40**, 287–309.

Christie, F. (ed.) (1990) *Literacy for a Changing World.* Melbourne: ACER.

Cochran-Smith, M. (1984) *The Making of a Reader.* Norwood, NJ: Ablex.

Cole, M. (1985) The zone of proximal development: where culture and cognition create each other. In J. R. Wertsch (ed.), *Culture, Communication, and Cognition: Vygotskian Perspectives.* Cambridge: Cambridge University Press.

Collerson, J. (ed.) (1988) *Writing for Life.* Sydney: Primary English Teaching Association.

Cooper, S. (1988) Preserving the light. *Magpies* **2** (May).

Corcoran, B. and Evans, E. (eds) (1987) *Readers, Texts, Teachers.* Upper Montclair, NJ: Boynton/Cook.

Crawford, M. (1993) *The Literacy Challenge.* Report of the House of Representatives Standing Committee on Employment, Education and Training. Canberra: Australian Government Publishing Service.

Davies, B. (1993) *Shards of Glass: Children Reading and Writing Beyond Gendered Identities.* Sydney: Allen & Unwin.

de Beaugrande, R. (1980) *Text, Discourse and Process.* Norwood, NJ: Ablex.

Delgado-Gaitan, C. (1991) Involving parents in schools: a process of empowerment. *American Journal of Education* **100**, 20–45.

Delgado-Gaitan, C. (1992) School matters in the Mexican-American home: socializing children to education. *American Educational Research Journal* **29**, 495–516.

Department of Education and Science (1967) *Children and Their Primary Schools: A Report of the Central Advisory Council for Education (England),* vol. 1: *Report* and vol. 2: *Research and Surveys* (Plowden Report). London: HMSO.

Department of Employment, Education and Training (1992) *Putting Literacy on the Agenda.* Canberra: DEET.

Derewianka, B. (1990) *Exploring How Texts Work.* Sydney: PETA.

Dillon, J. T. (1982) The multidisciplinary study of questioning. *Journal of Educational Psychology* **74** (2).

Dixon, J. (1967) *Growth Through English.* London: Oxford University Press.

Dyson, A. H. (1985) Writing and the social lives of children. *Language Arts* **62** (6).

Dyson, A. H. (1989) *Multiple Worlds of Child Writers: Friends Learning to Write.* New York: Teachers College Press.

Dyson, A. H. (1993) *Negotiating a Permeable Curriculum: On Literacy, Diversity and the Interplay of Children's and Teachers' Worlds, or the Mystery of Eugenie and Mr Lincoln.* Concept Paper Series. Urbana, IL: National Council for the Teaching of English.

Eastman, P. D. (1960) *Are You My Mother?* London: Collins.

Eco, U. (1979) *The Role of the Reader: Explorations in the Semiotics of Text.* Bloomington, IN: Indiana University Press.

Edelsky, C. (ed.) (1991) *With Literacy and Justice for All: Rethinking the Social in Language and Education.* London: Falmer.

Education Department of South Australia (1991) *Literacy Assessment in Practice.* Adelaide: Education Department of South Australia.

Edwards, V. and Furlong, A. (1978) *The Language of Teaching: Meaning in Classroom Interaction*. London: Heinemann.

Ehrlich, S. and Rayner, K. (1981) Contextual effects on word perception and eye movements during reading. *Journal of Verbal Learning and Verbal Behaviour* **20**, 641–55.

Emig, J. (1971) *The Composing Processes of Twelfth Graders*. National Council for Teachers of English Research Report 13. Urbana, IL: NCTE.

Epstein, J. (1983) *Effects on Parents of Teacher Practices of Parent Involvement*. Baltimore: The Johns Hopkins University. Report No. 346, pp. 277–94.

Fernie, D., Davies, B., Kantor, R. and McMurray, P. (1993) Becoming a person in the preschool: creating integrated gender, school culture, and peer culture positionings. *Qualitative Studies in Education* **6**, 95–110.

Flanders, N. A. (1970) *Analyzing Teaching Behaviour*. Reading, MA: Addison-Wesley.

Floriani, A. (1993) Negotiating what counts: roles and relationships, texts and contexts, content and meaning. *Linguistics and Education* **5**, 241–74.

Freebody, P. and Luke, A. (1992) A socio-cultural approach: resourcing four roles as a literacy learner. In A. Watson and A. Badenhop (eds), *Prevention of Reading Failure*. Gosford: Ashton Scholastic, pp. 48–60.

Freire, P. and Macedo, D. (1987) *Literacy: Reading the Word and the World*. London: Routledge & Kegan Paul.

Gall, M. (1970) The use of questions in teaching. *Review of Educational Research* **40** (5).

Garfield, L. (1981) *Fair's Fair*. London: Macdonald Futura.

Gee, J. (1990) *Social Linguistics and Literacies: Ideology in Discourses*. London: Falmer.

Gilbert, P. (1989) *Writing, Schooling, and Deconstruction: From Voice to Text in the Classroom*. London: Routledge.

Gilbert, P. and Taylor, S. (1991) *Fashioning the Feminine: Girls, Popular Culture and Schooling*. Sydney: Allen & Unwin.

Giroux, H. (1983) *Theory and Resistance in Education*. London: Heinemann.

Goodman, K. S. (1965) A linguistic study of cues and miscues in reading. *Elementary English* **42**, 639–43.

Goodman, K. S. (1967) Reading: a psycholinguistic guessing game. *Journal of the Reading Specialist* **6**, 126–35.

Goodman, Y. (1978) Kidwatching: observing children in the classroom. *Journal of National Elementary Principals* **57** (4), 41–5.

Gough, P. B. (1972) One second of reading. In J. Kavanagh and I. Mattingly (eds), *Language by Ear and Eye*. Cambridge, MA: MIT Press, pp. 331–58.

Graff, H. (1987) *The Labyrinths of Literacy: Reflections on Literacy Past and Present.* New York: Falmer.

Graves, D. (1983) *Writing: Teachers and Children at Work.* Portsmouth, NH: Heinemann.

Graves, D. H. (1984) *A Researcher Learns to Write: Selected Articles and Monographs.* Portsmouth, NH: Heinemann.

Graves, M. F. and Clark, D. L. (1981) The effect of adjunct questions on high school low achievers' reading comprehension. *Reading Improvement* **18**.

Graves, D. and Giacobbe, M. E. (1984) Questions for teachers who wonder if their writers change. In D. H. Graves, *A Researcher Learns to Write: Selected Articles and Monographs.* Portsmouth, NH: Heinemann.

Green, J. L. (1979) Communicating with young children. *Theory into Practice* **18** (4).

Green, J. L. and Dixon, C. N. (1993) Talking knowledge into being: discursive and social practices in classrooms. *Linguistics and Education* **5**, 231–9.

Green, J. L. and Wallat, C. (eds) (1981) *Ethnography and Language in Educational Settings.* Norwood, NJ: Ablex.

Greene, B. (1974) *Summer of My German Soldier.* London: Hamish Hamilton.

Guba, E. and Lincoln, Y. (1981) *Effective Evaluation: Improving the Usefulness of Evaluation Results Through Responsive and Naturalistic Approaches.* San Francisco, CA: Jossey-Bass.

Gumperz, J. (1986) *Discourse Strategies.* New York: Cambridge University Press.

Gutierrez, K. D. (1993) How talk, context, and script shape context for learning: a cross-case comparison of journal sharing. *Linguistics and Education* **5**, 335–65.

Halliday, M. A. K. (1975) *Learning How to Mean: Explorations in the Development of Language.* London: Edward Arnold.

Halliday, M. A. K. (1978) *Language as Social Semiotic.* London: Edward Arnold.

Hancock, J., Turbill, J. and Cambourne, B. (1994) Assessment and evaluation of literacy learning. In S. Valencia, E. H. Hiebert and P. P. Afflerbach (eds), *Authentic Reading Assessment: Practices and Possibilities.* Newark, DE: International Reading Association.

Hanusheck, E. A. (1981) Throwing money at schools. *Journal of Policy Analysis and Management* **1**, 19–41.

Harding, D. W. (1972) The role of onlooker. In A. Cashdan (ed.), *Language in Education: A Source Book.* Milton Keynes: Open University Press.

Harry, B. (1992) An ethnographic study of cross-cultural communication with Puerto Rican-American families in the special education system. *American Educational Research Journal* **29**, 471–94.

Harste, J. C., Burke, C. and Woodward, V. (1980) *The Young Child as Writer-Reader and Informant.* Final report for National Institute for Education. Bloomington, IN: Indiana University.

Harste, J. C., Pierce, K. and Cairney, T. H. (1985) *The Authoring Cycle*. Portsmouth, NH: Heinemann.

Harste, J. C., Woodward, V. and Burke, C. (1984) *Language Stories and Literacy Lessons*. Portsmouth, NH: Heinemann.

Hartman, D. K. (1990) The intertextual links of eight able readers using multiple passages: a postmodern/semiotic/cognitive view of meaning making. Paper presented at the Annual Meeting of the National Reading Conference, Miami, FL. December.

Hartog, P. (1907) *The Writing of English*. Oxford: Oxford University Press.

Heap, J. (1980) What counts as reading? Limits to certainty in assessment. *Curriculum Inquiry* **10**, 265–92.

Heap, J. (1991) A situated perspective on what counts as reading. In C. Baker and A. Luke (eds), *Towards a Critical Sociology of Reading Pedagogy*. Philadelphia, PA: John Benjamins, pp. 103–39.

Heath, S. B. (1983) *Ways with Words: Language, Life, and Work in Communities and Classrooms*. New York: Cambridge University Press.

Heide, F. P. (1975) *The Shrinking of Treehorn*. Harmondsworth, Middlesex, UK: Penguin.

Heras, A. I. (1993) The construction of understanding in a sixth-grade classroom. *Linguistics and Education* **5**, 275–99.

Hill, S. (1990) *Read With Me*. Canberra: Department of Employment, Education and Training.

Hoetker, J. and Ahlbrand, W. P. (1969) The persistence of the recitation. *American Educational Research Journal* **6**.

Holdaway, D. (1972) *Independence in Reading*. Gosford, NSW: Ashton Scholastic.

Hutchings, M. (1985) What teachers are demonstrating. In J. Newman (ed.), *Whole Language in Use*. Portsmouth, NH: Heinemann.

Hutchins, P. (1976) *Don't Forget the Bacon!* Harmondsworth, Middlesex: Penguin.

Hutchinson, V. S. (1969) Three billy goats gruff. In B. Sideman (ed.), *The World's Best Fairy Stories*. Sydney: Reader's Digest.

Hyman, R. T. (1979) *Strategic Questioning*. Englewood Cliffs, NJ: Prentice-Hall.

Hymes, D. (1974) *The Foundations of Sociolinguistics: Sociolinguistic Ethnography*. Philadelphia: University of Philadelphia Press.

Illinois Literacy Resource Development Center (1990) *The Mechanics of Success for Families*. Rantoul, IL: Illinois Literacy Resource Development Center.

Iser, W. (1978) *The Act of Reading: A Theory of Aesthetic Response*. Baltimore: Johns Hopkins University Press.

Jackson, B. L., Krasnow, J. and Seeley, D. (1994) The League of Schools reaching out: a New York city cluster building family–school–community partnership. Paper presented to the American Educational Research Association Conference, New Orleans, 4–8 April.

Jacobs, J. (1969) The three little pigs. In B. Sideman (ed.), *The World's Best Fairy Stories*. Sydney: Reader's Digest.

Jencks, C., Smith, M., Acland, H., Bane, M. J., Cohen, D., Gentis, H., Heynes, B. and Michelson, S. (1972) *Inequality: A Reassessment of the Effect of Family and Schooling in America*. New York: Basic Books.

Johnson, T. and Louis, D. (1985) *Literacy Through Literature*. Melbourne: Methuen.

Just, M. A. and Carpenter, P. A. (1980) A theory of reading: from eye fixations to comprehension. *Psychological Review* **4**, 329–54.

Keifer, B. (1983) The responses of children in a combination first/second grade classroom to picture books in a variety of artistic styles. *Journal of Research and Development in Education* **16**.

Kemp, M. (1989) Social context of literacy. Proceedings of the 17th Annual Australian Reading Association Conference. Canberra: ARA.

Kristeva, J. (1980) *Desire in Language: A Semiotic Approach to Literature and Art*. Translated by T. Gora, A. Jardine and L. S. Roudiez. New York: Columbia University Press.

Kuhn, T. S. (1970) *The Structure of Scientific Revolutions*, 2nd edn. Chicago: Chicago University Press.

Lankshear, C. and Lawler, M. (1987) *Literacy, Schooling and Revolution*. London: Falmer.

Lemke, J. L. (1993) On not making literate Americans. *Education Australia* **19–20**.

Luke, A. (1988) *Literacy, Textbooks and Ideology*. London: Falmer.

Luke, A. (1993) Stories of social regulation: the micropolitics of classroom narrative. In B. Green (ed.), *The Insistence of the Letter: Literacy Studies and Curriculum Theorising*. London: Falmer.

Luke, A. and Luke, C. (eds) (1989) *Language, Authority and Criticism: Readings on the School Textbook*. London: Falmer.

McGaw, B. and Grotelueschen, A. (1972) Directions of the effect of questions in prose material. *Journal of Educational Psychology* **63**.

Macrorie, K. (1985) *Telling Writing*, 4th edn. Upper Montclair, NJ: Boynton/Cook.

Mahy, M. (1987) Joining the network. *Signal* (September), 151–60.

Markle, G. and Capie, W. (1976) The effect of the position of inserted questions on learning from an activity centred science module. *Journal of Research in Science Teaching* **13** (2).

Martin, J., Christie, F. and Rothery, J. (1987) Social processes in education: a reply to Sawyer and Watson (and others). In I. Reid (ed.), *The Place of Genre in Learning: Current Debates*. Geelong, Vic.: Deakin University Press.

Martin, N., D'Arcy, P., Newton, B. and Parker, R. (1976) *Writing and Learning Across the Curriculum*. London: Ward Lock.

Maturana, H. R. and Varella, F. J. (1987) *The Tree of Knowledge*. Boston: Shambhala.

Meek, M. (1991) *On Being Literate*. London: Bodley Head.

Meek, M., Armstrong, S., Austerfield, V., Graham, J. and Plackett, E. (1983) *Achieving Literacy: Longitudinal Studies of Adolescents Learning to Read*. London: Routledge & Kegan Paul.

Moffett, J. (1968) *Teaching the Universe of Discourse*. Boston, MA: Houghton Mifflin Co.

Moll, L. (1988) Some key issues in teaching Latino students. *Language Arts* **65**, 465–72.

Morgan, R. T. T. (1976) 'Paired reading' tuition: a preliminary report on a technique for cases of reading deficit. *Child Care, Health and Development* **2**, 13–28.

Moyer, J. R. (1965) An exploratory study of questioning in the instructional processes in selected elementary schools. Unpublished doctoral dissertation, Columbia University. Ann Arbor, MI: Michigan University Microfilms, 66–2661.

Murray, D. (1982) *Learning by Teaching*. Montclair, NJ: Boynton Cook.

Murray, D. (1984) *Write To Learn*. New York: Holt, Rinehart and Winston.

Nicholson, T. (1991) Do children read words better in context or in lists? A classic study revisited. *Journal of Educational Psychology* **83**, 444–50.

Nickse, R. (1993) A typology of family and intergenerational literacy programmes: implications for evaluation. *Viewpoints* **15**, 34–40.

NSW Government (1992) *Draft English K-6 Syllabus*. Sydney: Government Printer.

Oakes, J. (1985) *Keeping Track: How Schools Structure Inequality*. New Haven, CT: Yale University Press.

Painter, C. (1986) The role of interaction in learning to speak and learning to write. In C. Painter and J. Martin (eds), *Writing To Mean: Teaching Genres Across the Curriculum*. Applied Linguistics Association of Australia, Occasional Papers, No. 9.

Palincsar, A. and Brown, A. (1983) *Reciprocal Teaching of Comprehension-monitoring Activities* (Technical Report No. 269). Urbana, IL: Center for the Study of Reading.

Pearson, P. D. and Johnson, D. (1978) *Teaching Reading Comprehension*. New York: Holt, Rinehart and Winston.

Perfetti, C. A. (1985) *Reading Ability*. New York: Oxford University Press.

Probst, R. E. (1988) Dialogue with a text. *English Journal* **77** (1), 32–8.

Read, C. (1975) *Children's Categorization of Speech Sounds in English*. National Council for the Teaching of English Research Report No. 17. Urbana, IL: NCTE.

Reece, J. (1976) *Lester and Clyde*. Gosford, NSW: Ashton Scholastic.

Rickards, J. P. and Hatcher, C. W. (1976) Type of verbatim question interspersed in text: a new look at the position effect. *Journal of Reading Behaviour* **8**.

Rist, R. (1970) Student social class and teacher expectations. *Harvard Educational Review* **40**.

Rogoff, B. (1990) *Apprenticeship in Thinking: Cognitive Development in Social Context*. Oxford: Oxford University Press.

Rogoff, B. (1994) Developing understanding of the idea of communities of learners. Scribner Award address, American Educational Research Association, New Orleans, 4–8 April.

Rosenblatt, L. (1976) *The Reader, the Text, the Poem*. Carbondale, IL: Southern Illinois University Press.

Rothkopf, E. Z. (1966) Learning from written instructive materials: an exploration of the control of inspection behaviour by test-like events. *American Educational Research Journal* **3**.

Rothkopf, E. Z. (1972) Structural text features and the control of processes in learning from written materials. In R. O. Freedle and J. B. Carroll (eds), *Language Comprehension and the Acquisition of Knowledge*. Washington, DC: Winston.

Rutter, M., Tizzard, J. and Whitmore, K. (1970) *Education Health and Behaviour*. London: Longmans.

Saussure, F. de (1974) *A Course in General Linguistics*. London: Fontana.

Sawyer, W. and Watson, K. (1987) Questions of genre. In I. Reid (ed.), *The Place of Genre in Learning: Current Debates*. Geelong, Vic.: Deakin University Press.

Scardemalia, M. and Bereiter, C. (1983) The development of evaluative diagnostic and remedial capabilities in children's composing. In M. Martlew (ed.), *The Psychology of Written Language*. New York: John Wiley & Sons.

Schaefer, E. (1991) Goals for parent and future parent education: research on parental beliefs and behaviour. *Elementary School Journal* **91**, 239–47.

Schallert, D. L. (1982) The significance of knowledge: a synthesis of research related to schema theory. In W. Otto and S. White (eds), *Reading Expository Material*. New York: Academic Press.

Scribner, S. and Cole, M. (1981) *The Psychology of Literacy*. Cambridge, MA: Harvard University Press.

Seuss, Dr (1974) *There's a Wocket in my Pocket*. New York: Collins.

Shanahan, T. and Rodriguez-Brown, F. (1993) The theory and structure of a family literacy program for the Latino community. Paper presented at the American Educational Research Association Conference, Atlanta (USA), 12–16 April.

Shanklin, N. K. L.(1982) *Relating Reading and Writing: Developing a Transactional Theory of the Writing Process*. Monographs in Teaching and Learning 5. Bloomington, IN: Indiana University Press.

Shannon, P. (1989) *Broken Promises: Reading Instruction in Twentieth Century America*. Granby, MA: Bergin & Garvey.

Smith, F. (1971) *Understanding Reading: A Psycholinguistic Analysis of Reading and Learning to Read*. New York: Holt, Rinehart & Winston.

Smith, F. (1978) *Reading Without Nonsense*. New York: Harper and Row.

Smith, F. (1988) *The Literacy Club*. London: Heinemann.

Smith, N. B. (1970) Many faces of reading comprehension. *The Reading Teacher* **23** (3).

Snow, C. (1983) Literacy and language in the preschool years. *Harvard Educational Review* **53** (2), 165–87.

Stake, R. (1975) *Evaluating the Arts in Education: A Responsive Approach*. Columbus, OH: Merrill.

Stevens, R. (1912) The question as a measure of efficiency in instruction: a critical study of classroom practice. *Teachers College Contributions to Education* **48**.

Stratta, L., Dixon, J. and Wilkinson, A. (1973) *Patterns of Language*. London: Heinemann.

Street, B. (1984) *Literacy in Theory and Practice*. Cambridge: Cambridge University Press.

Stubbs, M. (1980) *Language and Literacy*. London: Routledge & Kegan Paul.

Stubbs, M. (1983) *Language, Schools and Classrooms*. London: Methuen.

Thomas, K. F. (1985) Early reading as a social interaction process. *Language Arts* **62** (5).

Thompson, W. W. (1985) Environmental effects on educational performance. *The Alberta Journal of Educational Psychology* **31**, 11–25.

Tierney, R. J. and Cunningham, J. W. (1984) Research on teaching reading comprehension. In P. D. Pearson, R. Barr, M. L. Kamil and P. Mosenthal (eds), *Handbook of Reading Research*. New York: Longman.

Tierney, R. and Pearson, P. D. (1983) Toward a composing model of reading. *Language Arts* **60**, 568–80.

Tizard, J., Schofield, W. and Hewison, J. (1982) Collaboration between teachers and parents in assisting children's reading. *British Journal of Educational Psychology* **52**, 1–15.

Topping, K. and McKnight, G. (1984) Paired reading – and parent power. *Special Education – Forward Trends* **11**, 112–15.

Topping, K. and Wolfendale, S. (eds) (1985) *Parental Involvement in Children's Reading*. Beckenham, UK: Croom Helm.

Turbill, J. (ed.) (1982) *No Better Way to Teach Writing*. Sydney: PETA.

Valencia, S., Hiebert, E. H. and Afflerbach, P. P. (eds) (1994) *Authentic Reading Assessment: Practices and Possibilities*. Newark, DE: International Reading Association.

Valencia, S.W., McGinley, W. and Pearson, P. D. (1990) Assessing reading and writing. In G. Duffy (ed.), *Reading in the Middle School*. Newark, DE: International Reading Association, pp. 124–53.

Valencia, S. and Pearson, P. D. (1987) Reading assessment: time for change. *The Reading Teacher* **40** (8), 726–32.

Vaughan, M. K. (1984) *Wombat Stew*. Sydney: Ashton Scholastic.

Vygotsky, L. (1978) *Mind in Society: The Development of Higher Psychological Processes*. Cambridge, MA: Harvard University Press.

Wagner, J. (1979) *Aranea*. Harmondsworth, Middlesex, UK: Penguin.

Walshe, R. D. (1981) *Every Child Can Write! Learning and Teaching Written Expression in the 1980s*. Sydney: PETA.

Welch, A. R. and Freebody, P. (1993) Introduction: explanations of the current international 'literacy crises'. In P. Freebody and A. Welch (eds) *Knowledge, Culture and Power: International Perspectives on Literacy as Policy and Practice*. London: Falmer.

Wells, G. (1986) *The Meaning Makers*. Portsmouth, NH: Heinemann.

Wiesendanger, K. D. and Wollenberg, J. P. (1978) Prequestioning inhibits third grader's reading comprehension. *The Reading Teacher* **31**, 9.

Wilen, W. W. (1982). *What Research Says to the Teacher – Questioning Skills for Teachers*. New York: National Education Association.

Wilhelm, H. (1985). *I'll Always Love You*. New York: Crown.

Wilkinson, A. (1986). *The Quality of Writing*. Milton Keynes: Open University Press.

Willinsky, J. (1990). *The New Literacy: Redefining Reading and Writing in Schools*. New York: Routledge.

Woodward, H. (1993) *Negotiated Evaluation*. Sydney: Primary English Teaching Association.

Name Index

Subject Index